# Core Beliefs
## Harnessing the Power

PETER BUROW

**Core Beliefs – Harnessing The Power**
**ISBN9 780992 513535**

NeuroPower
Level 2, 147 Coronation Drive
MILTON QLD 4064

# Contents

Core Beliefs are deep-seated perceptions that everyone has about the world in which we live, work and play.

Core Beliefs impact how we think, feel and behave as well as how we interact with other people and our general view of the world.

# Foreword

In the three decades that I have spent in corporate business I feel that I have encountered nearly every major issue that business could throw at me.

My early career was with US-based multinationals in the manufacturing sector, then in distribution, followed by sales and marketing. My hope in those days was that MBAs and similar postgraduate courses would have all the answers I needed. But, although they often produced very interesting and useful frameworks for me to use, many times they failed in producing the actual business outcomes I was seeking.

Either I was not applying them correctly or there was something missing. I was eventually to discover that it was the latter and, what's more, that the missing piece is a crucial aspect missing from many of the models being used to this day.

As my career developed, I was required to address even more complex issues with higher and higher demands.

For example, in my role as Global Director of Strategy and Marketing for a top international accounting and consulting firm I needed to develop and implement a global strategy that would positively reposition the firm in light of competitive mega mergers.

Negotiating the buy-in to the global strategy across teams in Asia, South America, Europe and the USA required out-of-the-box, on-the-fly strategic responses in a way that I never thought possible.

Once I learnt the basic truth that people from each country held core beliefs that helped dictate their attitudes and behaviour, it became clear that these had to be recognised and accommodated if we were to achieve the cultural and behavioural changes required for implementation of the new strategic plan across the organisation.

The key to discovering this was being introduced to the Core Beliefs framework by Peter Burow - then a consultant in behavioural change - in the late 1990s.

The first insight was how the framework applied to me - I began to appreciate how my emotional self could hijack any rational thinking process, especially when in stressful situations, or when triggered by 'non-conforming' others.

Experiencing the benefits of the framework first-hand improved self-understanding and self-management; the next step was to explore its application in my relationships, personally and professionally, with individuals or groups; I saw positive results there too.

It became clear to me that what those MBA courses were missing was a full understanding of the way the human brain worked; they assumed that we all behaved rationally all the time, had full access to all necessary information and were always capable of objective analysis. How wrong this is!

Understanding that people's behaviour is a product of many factors – one of them being their core beliefs – that will manifest themselves in different ways under different conditions, was a breakthrough in the way I was able to increase my influence in the corporate world.

It was the breakthrough that allowed me to favourably influence the stakeholders in the corporate takeover that I mentioned above.

Later, I was able to get similarly positive results with branding and customer engagement in the highly competitive banking marketplace where products are very similar and the competitive price range is narrow.

Peter helped me discover the optimum rational and emotional connection with the customer, enabling fine tuning of service delivery in terms of the value proposition and the way it was communicated via the brand promise. The end result was a huge leap in both brand equity and employee engagement.

In both cases Peter Burow's framework supplied the 'missing piece' that I needed to combine with all the business knowledge and experience I had built up from working with many leading organisations around the world.

I began to manage more and more employees and was now enabled to implement strategic change with an enhanced business model based on 'open architecture'. I was able not only to address the perceived 'negative' aspects of core beliefs but to leverage the perceived 'positive' aspects to create more agile organisations.

In fact, today I attribute many of my key business achievements to the integration of intrinsic perspectives into the strategic and operational plans for which I was responsible for developing and implementing.

Core Beliefs has given me a robust framework for managing the often 'alien' perspectives that exist within individuals and groups. It is even a framework that can be applied to friends and family.

Core beliefs are, of course, universal but different for each of us; an understanding of the importance of this and what it means should be part of our earliest education; emotional intelligence does not come anywhere close to providing the insight that Core Beliefs delivers.

Perhaps there should even be a new core subject in an MBA program?

Have a look 'under the bonnet' of Core Beliefs; you may be surprised at what you will find. Perhaps you'll find evidence to back up your intuitions or you may just find something that helps you better deal with life's issues and complexities.

Susan Hilary Nixon
NED and Principal of Strategic Conversations

# Introduction

## What are Core Beliefs?

Core Beliefs are deep-seated perceptions that everyone has about the world in which we live, work and play. Core Beliefs impact how we think, feel and behave as well as how we interact with other people and our general view of the world. They can influence everything we do from the type of car we buy and the sort of house we live in through to the life partner we choose. They can also impact our work life, influencing every decision we make in whatever role we may fulfill. It doesn't matter if you're a mail room operative or a Chief Executive Officer, the decisions you make in that role, irrespective of how important they may be, are influenced by your Core Beliefs.

The Core Beliefs each of us have are developed over many years through regular interaction with our family, friends, clients, colleagues and other reference sources such as the media, politicians and movies. The important thing about Core Beliefs is that they cannot be easily changed. What can be altered is the intensity with which we hold them.

This can be reduced or increased by the information others share with us, and how this information is communicated to us. From your point of view, your stakeholders' Core Beliefs fall into two types – anti-positional (disagree with your position) or pro-positional (agree with your position). For every pro-positional Core Belief there is a mirror-image anti-positional Core Belief.

## What classifies as a Core Belief?

Within our home, work and leisure activities, we all at some point in time *belong to a particular community*. It may be as a member of an *employee work team*, it may be as a *consumer*, it may be as a *driver*, it may be as a *parent*, it may be as a *Board member of a company*, it may be as a *member of a company's senior management group*.

The important factor here is membership of the community. This is important because it is only when 75 per cent of that community, whatever it may be, holds the same view that the particular belief can be classified as a Core Belief.

If less than 75 per cent of that community shares the same view, then it is not a Core Belief but just a collection of individual beliefs.

## The bandwagon effect

If a belief is held by more than 75 per cent of the community, research has shown that the power of this 75 per cent will automatically influence a further 15 per cent of the particular community to adopt the particular Core Belief. This is called the *bandwagon effect.*

This means that if you are seeking to influence a particular target audience and can successfully align your key messages with a Core Belief, you will end up with not just 75 per cent support but 90 per cent support because the bandwagon effect will give you an additional 15 per cent.

The bandwagon effect also works in reverse. If support for the belief falls just 1 below 75 per cent, support for that belief will lose the 15 per cent bandwagon support. This means that support for that belief will rapidly fall from 90 per cent to 74 per cent.

## Example of a Core Belief

The statement 'smoking is bad for your health' is a Core Belief which can be both anti-positional and pro-positional.

For example the statement 'smoking is bad for your health' is anti-positional to the smoking lobby and cigarette manufacturers. In contrast, it is pro-positional to the health lobby and a large proportion of the general public who oppose smoking.

An equally strong but opposite Core Belief to the above statement is 'we should all have the freedom to smoke if we want'. This Core Belief is pro-positional to the smoking lobby and cigarette manufacturers but anti-positional to the health lobby and a large proportion of the general public who oppose smoking.

## How Core Beliefs are formed

Based on many years' research, there is global consensus that each of us relies on one of nine different processes to develop our Core Beliefs. Each of these processes is dependent on a number of factors including our individual personalities as well as how we react to specific situations and events when placed under decision-making stress.

The nature of our response to the emotional stress associated with making a decision will tend to follow specific patterns. These patterns for an evoked set[1] of behavioural patterns can be tracked over time. It is upon these behavioural patterns that the characteristics used to profile each Core Belief group has been empirically tested.

These emotional stresses arise when we translate anything outside our control to one of three emotional reactions: fight, flight or compliance (another way to look at it is the emotions of anger, fear or approval-seeking).

Over the course of our life we have developed a series of survival mechanisms designed to respond, unthinkingly, to these strong emotions. David Chalmers referred to these judgements as first order judgements.

These evoked sets are created to enhance the brain's capacity to deal with the adverse environmental stimuli, thereby enhancing evaluative capacity and strategies for dealing with the problem. Each of these emotional states carries with it a distinct set of drivers, or positional feelings and beliefs. These drivers substantially determine the components of the evoked set that underlies a Core Belief.

There are nine generic defensive strategies that individuals use and each has a distinct set of drivers. These unique drivers bring with them explicit perceptual filters that determine what we pay attention to and how energy is directed. Underneath each of the nine patterns is a basic proposition, or belief, about what we need in life for survival and satisfaction, and the unconscious motivation from which we operate. These Core Beliefs are summarised on the opposite page and explained more fully in Chapter Two.

The Core Beliefs model tracks and predicts an individual's responsive behaviours based on the emotive evoked set. This model has been statistically validated as a typology through the work of Dr Jerome Wagner.

---

1   In 1963 John A. Howard of Columbia University, a marketing scholar, developed the concept of an evoked set to describe an individual's emotive response to stimuli.

---

# Core Beliefs Model

**Core Belief Profile 1 – Perfectionists** *Focus: Integrity/Clarity*

They believe you must be good and right to be worthy. Consequently, they are conscientious, responsible, improvement-oriented and self-controlled, but also can be critical, resentful and self-judging.

**Core Belief Profile 2 – Helpers** *Focus: Influence*

They believe you must give fully to others to be loved. Consequently, they are caring, helpful, supportive and relationship-oriented, but also can be prideful, overly intrusive and demanding.

**Core Belief Profile 3 – Achievers** *Focus: Achieving Results*

They believe you must accomplish and succeed to be loved. Consequently, they are industrious, fast-paced, goal-focused and efficiency-oriented, but also can be inattentive to feelings, impatient and image-driven.

**Core Belief Profile 4 – Artists** *Focus: Elite Standards*

They believe you must obtain the longed-for ideal relationship or situation to be loved. Consequently, they are idealistic, deeply feeling, empathetic and authentic to self, but also dramatic, moody and sometimes self-absorbed.

**Core Belief Profile 5 – Analysts** *Focus: Analysis/Depth of Technical Knowledge*

They believe you must protect yourself from a world that demands too much and gives too little to assure life. Consequently, they are self-sufficiency seeking, non-demanding, analytical/thoughtful and unobtrusive, but also can be withholding, detached and overly private.

**Core Belief Profile 6 – Loyal Sceptics** *Focus: Loyalty/Scepticism*

They believe you must gain protection and security in a hazardous world you just can't trust. Consequently, they are themselves trustworthy, inquisitive, good friends and questioning, but also can be overly doubtful, accusatory and fearful.

**Core Belief Profile 7 – Epicures** *Focus: New Opportunities*

They believe you must keep life up and open to assure a good life. Consequently, they are optimistic, upbeat, possibility- and pleasure-seeking and adventurous, but also can be pain-avoidant, uncommitted and self-serving.

**Core Belief Profile 8 – The Boss** *Focus: All or Nothing*

They believe you must be strong and powerful to assure protection and regard in a tough world. Consequently, they are justice-seeking, direct, strong and action-oriented, but also overly impactful, excessive and sometimes impulsive.

**Core Belief Profile 9 – Peacemakers** *Focus: Minimising Conflict*

They believe that to be loved and valued you must blend in and go along to get along. Consequently, they are self-forgetting, harmony-seeking, comfortable and steady, but also conflict avoidant and sometimes stubborn.

# CHAPTER ONE
# The Formation of Core Beliefs

The world is far too rich with stimuli to assess each and every one in making a decision so we adopt perceptual short cuts. These short cuts act as filters and provide easy assessments of information. For example, in the average shopping expedition you are confronted with over 25,000 options, far too many to rationally assess and evaluate each and every product! Since we actually make very few choices, and leave with only a (relatively) few products, we tend to rely on relatively simple evaluations to arrive at our decisions and then to retrospectively justify them. It would be impossible to evaluate each and every option by assessing all the available information and carefully evaluate it in reaching a decision.

**We use Core Beliefs to simplify our decision-making process.** There are two broad methods in making a decision, either through:

- affect (an emotionally driven approach); or
- logic (a cognitive approach) according to marketing researcher Milton Holbrook (1976).

The cognitive approach to decision-making involves assessing all inputs and considerations in making an evaluation. It involves relating current information with previous knowledge stored in the memory and generating new implications for yourself, while also reconciling internal conflicts that result from living in a world where resources (like time and money) are limited.

Limited resources mean we all have desires that will not be satisfied or sated and these must be assessed, prioritised and evaluated in any given decision.

Obviously, this is too cumbersome, or simply too difficult, for the majority of decisions we face on a daily basis.

When we are unable or unwilling to make the mental effort required in a cognitive decision, we tend to use relatively simple cues to arrive at conclusions, or relatively simple positions to justify a decision (an affect decision).

Core Beliefs represent the cues that we use to simplify both the information we receive and our own decision-making process. So, while Core Beliefs short cuts represent perceptions about the world, it is also helpful to think of them as simplifications used to justify resolving internal conflict.

While we are all different, our differences have close similarities. In particular, there are strong similarities amongst the different emotional drivers that cause internal conflict and these form the nine Core Belief Profiles. Each of these Core Belief Profiles will experience unique internal conflict (as they assess and experience the environment through subtly different ways), but will respond with similar Core Belief statements to justify a decision.

Consider the example of John 4:4, 'A prophet has no honour in his own country.'

This ancient Bible verse is a current Core Belief that for an idea to have merit and be worthwhile (or to be truly 'inspired') it must come from a source far, far away. The relatively simple process that people use to assess the validity of an individual is to assess where the individual comes from, rather than the content and accuracy of the idea itself. Our perceptions of a nation, city or location will influence our evaluations of the concepts being presented to us.

The universality of Core Beliefs within any community is explained through chaos theory and psychological critical point analysis. With the advent of advanced computers, vast amounts of data could be graphically depicted, revealing consistent systems (Lorenz, 1963). Theoreticians were suddenly able to discover coherent ways of understanding data that had been considered incoherent, or non-linear, that were not possible through classical (linear) physics. Analysis of this 'incoherent' data reveals hidden energy patterns, or attractors behind apparently random natural phenomena (Mandelbrot, 1977).

Essentially, chaos refers to the phenomenon wherein systems composed of interrelated parts or interdependent agents – each of which follows very simple, highly regular rules of behaviour – generate outcomes that reflect these interactions and feedback effects in ways that are inherently non-linear and intractably unpredictable. Because of the non-linearities that reflect interactions and feedback effects, very tiny changes in inputs can make enormous differences in outputs, like the so-called butterfly effect in which, for example, the proverbial butterfly flapping its wings in Brazil can cause a tornado in Texas. Potentially, systems can spin towards various sorts of attractor states where a form of stability is achieved.

Core Beliefs represent psychologically critical points at which different people, assessing different information and with different backgrounds, will arrive at the same conclusion. Critical point analysis is a technique derived from the fact that in any highly complex system there is a specific critical point at which the smallest input will result in the greatest change. The gears of a large windmill can be halted through the lightest touch on the right mechanism. In a similar fashion, Core Beliefs can provide you with tremendous capacity to shape opinion and decision-making since they are the tiny gears around which opinions swing.

Neuro-physiological modelling, that applies the theories of non-linear dynamics to brain function, has found attractor networks in the brain. The conclusions of current research are that the brain's neural networks act as a system of attractor patterns (Li and Spiegel, 1992). Neuron models have disclosed a class of neural networks called *constrain satisfaction systems*. In these systems a network of interconnected neuron units operates within a series of limits and thus sets up attractor patterns, some of which are now being identified with psychopathology (Hoffman, 1992).

Core Beliefs represent a series of attractor networks that the brain relies on when it is unable or unwilling to maintain the tension between various drivers.

While they are influenced by our unique motivations and life experiences, they form recurring patterns that are both highly predictable and highly consistent. Meeting a stranger is a good example of the role Core Beliefs play in simplifying decision-making. Research (Tracy, 2004) has found that we tend to draw a firm judgement about a person within 30 seconds of meeting them.

This is not a very long time in which to have reached a cognitive evaluation of them and so we tend to rely on *cues* to assess them.

Once we have reached a *conclusion*, we start justifying our conclusions about the individual. Consider meeting an obese and sweaty man for the first time. Many would typically think, 'He is an individual with no self-control (to allow himself to become so fat)' and then start looking for corroborating evidence of his lack of self-control. Rather than logically piecing together the evaluation to form a conclusion we use Core Beliefs to reach the conclusion and then collect data and justify our point of view. This process is called a self-justifying reframe of empirical data.

## Characteristics of Core Beliefs

There are vastly different characteristics between a cognitive decision and an affect driven decision. These arise from the different aspects of the brain that are used in the decision-making process. The cognitive process is centered in the neocortex (which allows us to think about thinking) while Core Beliefs arise from the amygdala (which acts like an internal watchdog scanning the environment for threats). The differences between these two areas of the brain give rise to a number of important characteristics about Core Beliefs.

These are:

- Core Beliefs cannot be changed because they are based on a chemical or instinctual reaction (except slowly, over a great deal of time);
- Focusing on one Core Belief can alter the intensity with which another Core Belief is held;
- Core Beliefs are not closely related to facts;
- Core Beliefs are strongly (but irrationally) held;
- The degree to which people rely on Core Beliefs to make a decision can be influenced; and
- Core Beliefs tend to be subconscious and the cognitive mind is used to justify rather than question them.

In contrast, when we attempt to resolve our disparate internal drives through a cognitive process, then the decisions tend to be:

- Relatively easy to call to mind;
- Relatively persistent and stable; and
- Relatively resistant to challenges from other ideas or messages.

Consider the position of an individual sitting at home watching the television when a political advertisement plays. This patriotic Australian is an undecided voter and also fairly indifferent to the political process (if there is no imminent election looming). When an advertisement appears with a politician draped in an Australian flag, the individual does not pay it cognitive attention. Instead, if they see the Australian flag and associate that with their own patriotism they will arrive at a position that the politician would consider to be pro-positional.

If our imaginary patriot had been watching the television with active interest in the political process, they may have made a deeper assessment of the advertisement. They may well have considered the message of the advertisement in terms of their own political, religious and social views to arrive at a conclusion about the politician's political position. This decision is likely to be stronger and longer lasting than a decision based solely on external cues.

## Internal conflicts and the Core Belief Profiles

When people do not use their cognitive abilities to arrive at a personal decision (to resolve their own inner conflicts), they collapse into one of nine predictable patterns of Core Belief Profile behaviour. These nine Core Belief Profiles arise from nine separate internal drivers. While each of us has a tendency towards one or the other of these nine profiles (our temperament), each profile forms around a signature emotion.

While the emotion itself will typically be of a short but intense duration, each temperament will have a typical mood that colours its perceptions and behaviours. For example, an individual in a 'bad' mood is far more likely to become angry about an issue or occurrence that happens in the course of a day than an individual who is in a happy mood. If the individual Core Belief Profile formed around anger, they will start recognising issues to justify/trigger their anger in their environment. Core Beliefs will be used by their neocortex to justify their current feelings and expressions of feelings (self-justifying reframe). The degree to which an individual's behaviour aligns with a Core Belief Profile will be determined by the degree to which an individual has allowed the environmental stressors to dictate their mood. For example, if the individual mentioned previously had one of the Core Belief Profiles based around the emotion of anger, they will respond with behaviour

# The decision-making process

There are two systems at work in the brain: System 1 is the Intuitive or Emotional Brain and System 2 is the Rational Brain.

The Intuitive or Emotional Brain is where our Core Beliefs reside and relates to our intuitive response to outside happenings which result in fight, flight and freeze. Our responses and decisions are fast, automatic, unconscious and difficult to control or modify. This part of our brain gives only partial understanding.

The Rational Brain relates to our reasoning, conscious part of the brain. Our decisions here are slow, considered, rule-governed and controlled, and give a more complete understanding.

We need to understand both these modes and their influence on judgements and choice, as they are the key to behavioural change.

SYSTEM 1 - INTUITIVE BRAIN

- Fast
- Automatic
- Effortless
- Associative
- Difficult to control or modify
- Uses feeling
- Imagination rules
- 'Big picture' oriented
- Spatial perception
- Presents possibilities
- Risk-taking
- Core Beliefs

SYSTEM 2 - RATIONAL BRAIN

- Slow
- Serial
- Effortful
- Rule-governed
- Controlled
- Uses logic
- Detail-oriented
- Facts rule
- Order/pattern perception
- Forms strategies
- Safe

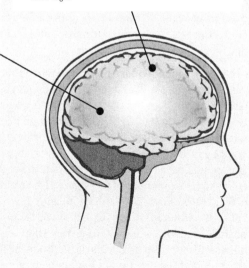

that aligns with three Core Belief Profiles: Core Belief Profile One, Core Belief Profile Eight or Core Belief Profile Nine.

The degree to which they do not cognitively assess their decision-making process will indicate the degree to which they rely upon Core Beliefs. The psychologist Richard Wenzlaff states, "Thoughts are associated in the mind not just by content, but by mood. People have what amounts to a set of bad mood thoughts that come to mind more readily when they are feeling down."

In a series of experiments volunteers were told heart-wrenching scenarios of tragedy and were then asked to try and distract themselves with other thoughts. Volunteers who were already depressed would try and distract themselves with other distressing thoughts.

The Core Belief Profiles are based around emotional states generated in the amygdala. The amygdala is part of our more primitive centre for interpreting our environmental stimuli. The primary function of the amygdala is to scan the environment for potentially hostile inputs and to arrive at an immediate response. This is a role that it plays in all animals and forms the same function of interpreting hostile events and determining whether to fight, to run away, or to comply with the threat (flight, fight or freeze).

Consider a dog's response to an angry owner who is threatening to hit it. The dog can either fight, it can run away, or it can crawl on its belly and fawn. A dog's amygdala presents it with three responses. In the case of humans, the amygdala is relatively large and provides greater variety in responses.

Specifically, there are still only three general responses to perceived threats, but there are three different ways to fight, run away or to comply. These nine approaches give rise to the Core Belief Profiles. They will be discussed in more detail later with a chapter devoted to each.

The reason that the amygdala plays such a powerful role in interpreting and evaluating our environment is because of its purpose in our personal survival. Since it prompts us to action through chemically inducing emotion[2], it acts as a storehouse of all emotional memory. All passion and emotion depends on the amygdala as it stores emotional associations.

---

2    The root of the word is in the Latin verb 'to move' with the prefix 'e-' to connote 'move away' suggesting that there is a tendency to act implicitly in every emotion.

One young man who had his amygdala surgically removed (to control severe seizures) became completely uninterested in other people. While he was capable of conversation, he no longer recognised close friends, relatives, or even his own mother (Joseph, 1993). Without an amygdala he seemed to have lost all recognition of feeling, as well as any feeling about feeling. Further, animals that have had their amygdala removed or severed, lack fear or rage and lose the urge to compete or cooperate.

Research by neuroscientist Joseph LeDoux explains how the amygdala can take control over what we do even as the thinking brain (the neocortex) is still coming to a decision. Incoming signals from the senses allow the amygdala to scan every experience for trouble. The amygdala evaluates every moment, 'Is this something that I hate? That hurts me? Something I fear?' If the answer is yes, their amygdala will react instantaneously, transmitting a message of crisis to all parts of the brain.

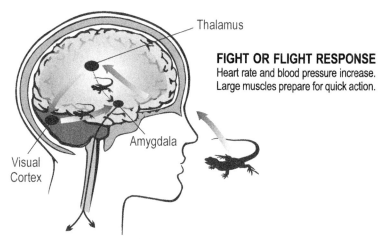

Thalamus

**FIGHT OR FLIGHT RESPONSE**
Heart rate and blood pressure increase.
Large muscles prepare for quick action.

Amygdala

Visual
Cortex

Psychologists refer to these perceived threats as stressors and they are specific things that put either physical or psychological pressure on an individual. If the amygdala interprets a stressor as something to be feared, then it will trigger the secretion of the body's fight-or-flight hormones, mobilise the centres for movement and activate the cardiovascular system, the muscles and the gut (Kagan, 1994). LeDoux's research reveals that the amygdala receives some direct inputs from the senses and can start responding before they are fully registered in the neocortex.

The interval between what triggers an emotion and its eruption can be virtually instantaneous. The chemical states, or emotions, that the amygdala creates to handle stressors are the key to Core Beliefs. They represent the emotions that the amygdala has triggered to resolve a specific stimuli in the environment. Since these chemicals are not removed completely from the system, they represent moods that last for much longer periods of time and that will predispose the person to act in set ways to the stimuli.

The degree to which Core Beliefs determine decision-making is dictated by the degree to which either a mood or an emotion determines what information is assessed through a cognitive process. Holbrook and Batra (1987) found that the affective (emotionally-driven) element of decision-making comprised three broad drivers. These three broad dimensions of emotions are similar to the three categories of Core Belief Profiles. Core Belief Profiles form with a tendency to express one emotion because the same chemicals that the brain uses to create a physical response to the environment are also the same ones that potently embed the event in memory (Cahill, L., et al., 1994).

Therefore, what has caused a strong reaction in the past is most likely to draw a reaction in the future. These responses become hardwired into the brain because as you scan and see the same particular threat, it tends to become a lot more prevalent as the neural patterns become more frequently accessed, and hence more accessible.

These three broad categories of issues that form the basis of threats perceived within the amygdala are the basis of the Core Belief Profiles. They are:
- Attention – which plays out as a focus on relationships;
- Security – which plays out as a focus on intellectual answers; and
- Individual autonomy – which plays out as a focus on physical issues.

These categories align with the work of psychiatrist Karen Horney who identified three fundamental ways in which people interact in a social setting.

This work was based on the earlier work of Sigmund Freud on how people attempt to resolve their internal conflicts. These three styles represent the social approach of the Core Belief Profiles and the manner in which they externalise their inner conflicts. The three basic approaches are:

1. Assertive about resolving their internal conflicts in the external domain. These types are ego-oriented and ego-expansive and they respond to stress or difficulty by building up, reinforcing or inflating their egos.
2. Compliant by needing to be of service to other people. These types respond to stressors by complying in the belief that this will remove the perceived stressors.
3. Withdrawal from social interactions and from issues that threaten the broad issues about which they are focused. These types respond to stress by withdrawing into an internal world.

These three categories represent three ways people respond to stressors and seek to answer the inner cries of their amygdala and its warnings of danger.

Breaking reactive responses into the Horneyian triad forms an efficient basis for Core Belief research. This is very important in predicting how individuals will respond to situations and seek to 'resolve' their own unique issues of existence.

## The amygdala and the neocortex

While the Core Belief Profiles are based around emotions, emotions can arise from either the amygdala (the reactive part of the brain) or the neocortex (the thinking part of the brain). The neocortex allows us to comprehend what our senses perceive.

Therefore the neocortex is the centre of thought. It adds to a feeling what we think about it – while we may feel fear because of a certain object, the neocortex allows us to think and reason why we have that fear. It allows for the subtlety and complexity in emotional life such as the ability to have feelings about our feelings. It also explains the wider variety of responses that humans can have with their environment since we have so much more thinking capacity – in fact, the human brain is roughly triple the size of our nearest evolutionary relatives.

The emotions that arise in the neocortex can be controlled and rationally assessed. It is a more deliberate emotional route, as we are typically aware of the thoughts that lead to it. This is clearly demonstrated in an actor's capacity to cry on demand by thinking about sad memories.

The actor is consciously aware that they are focusing on elements in their environment (namely their brain) that will generate a specific response. The emotional experiences of our neocortex are capable of being assessed, evaluated and revised.

In contrast to this controlled perception of the environment, emotions generated out of the amygdala are very strong and have clear physical consequences. Chemicals are released into the body in order to deal with the environment; these are then interpreted as emotions.

All strong and reactive emotions are impulses to action since they chemically prime the body to be prepared to take specific actions. For example, when someone is angry, then blood flows to the hands, which would make it easier to strike an opponent or to pick up a weapon. Also, the heart rate increases and a rush of hormones, like adrenaline, generate a strong pulse of energy with which to attack another.

Likewise, when the emotion of fear occurs then blood goes to the large skeletal muscles, such as in the legs, making it easier to flee. Circuits in the brain's emotional centres trigger a flood of hormones that put the body on general alert, making it edgy and ready for action, and attention fixates on the threat at hand.

## Unconscious reactions

"Some emotional reactions and emotional memories can be formed without any conscious, cognitive participation at all," stated LeDoux. The amygdala can house memories and response repertoires that we enact without quite realising why we do so because the neocortex can be completely bypassed.

This means we can have emotional connections and reactions to objects that we have no conscious awareness of and explains the formation of evoked sets described by John A. Howard. For example, people can have preferences for geometric figures that had been flashed at them so quickly that they had no conscious awareness of having seen them at all (Kunst-Wilson, et. al. 1980).

Emotional preferences and evaluation can arise from this unthinking side of the brain, the amygdala. This means we can have formed emotional responses to stimuli we are not consciously aware of. We will never question an association we do not know that we have made.

## Speedy but inaccurate assessments

The emotional associations made in the amygdala represent the central core of the formation of evoked sets and Core Beliefs. As the repository for emotional memory, the amygdala scans experience, comparing what is happening now with what happened in the past. Its method of comparison is associative: when a key element of a present situation is similar to the past, it can call it a match and will respond accordingly.

Therefore, what something reminds us of will be more important than what it is and it only needs one part of an identity to evoke the whole memory.

So the amygdala will make connections between things that merely have similar striking features (Epstein, 1993). These associations will represent inaccurate linkages, as they will be based on partial matches and incomplete assessments. Since the emotional intensity of these associations is not brought into the rational mind for consideration, they are not questioned as to their accuracy. Therefore, these drivers and interpretations of the world will be acting as subconscious filters, altering perceptions and setting priorities on a purely subconscious level.

This helps explain the inaccuracy of Core Beliefs, as the circuitry of the amygdala can become engaged in generating a response before all the information about a situation has been assessed. This occurs because the amygdala is primed to ensure survival – and this requires fast responses to threatening environments. When survival depends on recognising danger and responding to it immediately, the analysis of the neocortex is a detrimental ability. While most people face few, if any, situations in which this survival skill is necessary, we all have it hardwired into our brains.

## Core Beliefs are fixed

The emotional connections that the brain makes are fixed in that as the amygdala scans the environment for stressors, it will make connections to events and situations with those it considers similar to past occasions. So when an event seems similar to an emotionally charged memory, the mind responds by triggering the feelings that went with that event. This leads to disproportionate reactions to symbols, statements or events that trigger the amygdala's fight/flight/comply mechanism.

Part of the mind's response to a stressful situation is to reshuffle memory and options for action so that those most relevant are at the top of the hierarchy and so more readily enacted. This makes emotional states self-justifying, with a set of perceptions and 'proofs' all their own. That is, each chemical reaction is state-based and so only information that supports it is recognised. Part of the reason for this is that the amygdala does not have a great deal of connection with the rest of the brain, and is almost shorn from it.

Therefore, it only remembers/looks at information that supports its position (in the present or in the past) and minimises other information (Wenzlaff, 1993).

## Certainty of Core Beliefs

Not only do Core Beliefs summarise the environment, they also provide an enormous sense of clarity and 'rightness'. The stronger the emotion or chemical state grows, then the more categorical and clear thinking seems. As the amygdala releases chemicals that focus on the perceived threat, this threat becomes the centre of attention, and so it tends to grow clearer and more absolute.

This can be best illustrated with a survival situation. Think of the tunnel vision of a rabbit being hunted by a dog. The rabbit's senses focus on seeking a means of escape, so its eyes will dilate and it will enter what feels like a heightened level of awareness. The physical state will allow it to better sense the danger and run faster to get away from that danger. This means that data that is irrelevant to a rabbit being chased – like 'that looks like nice grass to eat' which will not be pertinent if the rabbit dies – will be ignored.

The clarity that Core Beliefs provide is not unlike the last stages of syphilis. In fact, the process of contracting syphilis is not unlike the formation of Core Beliefs. In the first stage of syphilis, the disease is an irritation to the body as it initially infects the host with a rash around sensitive body parts.

The emotions that Core Beliefs are formed around are initially very annoying and sharp. This discomfort is not maintained as the chemical levels subside to create a mood. In syphilis, in the second stage of the disease it appears as if it has gone into remission. While the irritation leaves, the disease is actually permeating the entire body. In the final stage of syphilis the host feels that they have great clarity about the world and a strong sense of certainty.

Unfortunately, this certainty is caused by brain damage and has the price of death. Core Beliefs offer a great sense of clarity as they focus the attention purely on the supporting data and eliminate the annoying need to think about contrary information, but this great clarity does not necessarily represent reality.

## Your Core Beliefs will kill you

Each Core Belief Profile is based around a different set of chemical states that the amygdala releases. The Core Belief Profiles represent temperaments with a strong tendency to experience certain emotions most often. This means that a range of chemicals is continually inundating the body, with long-term side effects. Let us return to our chased rabbit.

The perception of a dangerous or frightening situation causes the release of chemicals, called neurotransmitters, from the pituitary gland. These chemicals impact on many tissues in the rabbit's body, but most notably the adrenal glands.

Consequently, in the short term the rabbit's respiratory rate increases, its eyes dilate and its blood sugar levels soar. If these chemicals are maintained for a long period of time, they affect the rabbit negatively. The restriction of blood supply to not-immediately-essential areas leads to their deterioration, and the exhaustion of the liver's energy stores (required to maintain the heightened state of awareness) can lead to a starvation of body tissues that is lethal. In rabbits this leads to shock disease where the rabbit's body collapses after being exposed to stressful circumstances for a prolonged period of time.

A similar process of deterioration occurs in humans. Which set of chemicals is released will influence the likelihood of different diseases affecting the individual. There has been considerable work done in determining the correlations between the Core Belief Profiles and the emotions that they are based upon.

# Commercially speaking

We are exposed to too many environmental stimuli every day to make rational decisions. Instead, we tend to screen out the vast majority of information and perceive only what is of interest to us. In determining what is of interest to us, we will tend to rely on Core Beliefs as environmental cues to focus our attention.

Research by Reis and Trout (2000) has found that the majority of customers identify a product or company in terms of only one characteristic or attribute. Unless this particular characteristic is of relevance to them (that is, it addresses a Core Belief association that is desirable to them) customers are unlikely to make a purchase.

Unless your message agrees with the Core Beliefs of the community, it will not penetrate the perceptual filters we all employ. Therefore, to have effective and persuasive communication requires an understanding of the Core Beliefs that are associated with your position.

# Core Belief articulation

The link between the Core Belief and the emotion is not explicit. It is an implicit connection that individuals make between their own internal drivers and the Core Belief.

When each of the Core Belief Profiles are asked, 'Is democracy good?' they will respond 'Yes!' (if it forms a Core Belief of their community). One Core Belief Profile will think so because it allows a wide range of options and anything that limits their options is bad and must be avoided.

Another Core Belief Profile will feel democracy is good because their uniqueness can only be appreciated in an environment that encourages and allows people to be unique. In neither case will they have assessed the overall social benefit of democracy, the various historical and economic factors that are required for it to be effective, or any issue requiring cognitive thought.

While the underlying motivations will differ, each of the nine Core Belief Profiles will respond, 'I am for democracy.' In other words, the nine Core Belief types may all answer 'Yes' but for completely different reasons. These will be explored in more detail in the following chapter.

# CHAPTER TWO
# The Nine Core Belief
# Profiles

## Core Belief Profile One – Perfectionists

Core Belief Profile One has a strong need to be considered a good person and their emotional drivers are to do what is perceived as right and good in their community. They live by extremely high personal standards of excellence, and expect others to do so as well. The Core Belief Profile One personality focuses on living the one right way. This stems from an assumption that there is one ultimately correct solution for every situation. Core Belief Profile Ones are dedicated to this one right way as a statement of character, regardless of how attractive other ways might be. They also seek to improve themselves and others since they want to be right and to justify their position and to be beyond criticism and reproach.

The reason that they have high standards is because they feel that they must gain a sense of worthiness (love) through being good, correcting error and being responsible. Core Belief Profile One is a compliant profile since it seeks affirmation through being good, correcting error and being responsible. This means that they seek to embody socially acceptable standards and behaviours.

They seek autonomy through strict adherence to the social rules, and through imposing them on other people.

### Emotional state

The Core Belief Profile One is formed around the emotion of anger because nothing is as it should be. This is a dilemma since anger itself is bad and must be avoided by the good boy or good girl. Ones do not acknowledge their own resentment until they are absolutely certain that they are in the right and then they express their anger as self-righteous indignation. This self-righteous anger is often an externalisation of their preoccupation with being correct so that they

# Principal Characteristics – Profile One

### Focus of attention
- What is right and wrong. They are particularly concerned with what is wrong so that it can be corrected
- The rightness and wrongness of other people's behaviour in comparison to their own
- Self-criticism and criticism from others

(Adapted from Daniels, et. al. 2000, p22)

### Focus of energy
- Getting things right
- Issues about integrity
- Maintaining standards judged to be important
- Being responsible and self-reliant
- Suppressing personal needs and natural desires

(Adapted from Daniels, et. al. 2000, p22)

### Focus of avoidance
- Making mistakes
- Being aggressive
- Losing self-control
- Violating social norms

(Adapted from Daniels, et. al. 2000, p22)

### Self-justifying reframes
- Integrity
- Concern for improvement
- Putting forth a lot of effort
- Idealism
- Self-reliance
- Industriousness
- Keeper of high standards
- Self-restraint
- Being highly responsible

### Weakness
- Resentment
- Judgement

### Preferred communication style
- Prefers clear directions with lots of definition and structure
- Needs to understand things thoroughly before moving on; new information should come in manageable pieces and at a steady pace
- Likes to narrow the focus and cover all the angles; often uncomfortable with open-ended material
- Wants to be able to learn/do things correctly, even if that means going slowly
- Wants the instructor/manager to be competent and socially correct

### Key words and traits
- Anger
- Criticality
- Demanding
- Dominance
- Perfectionism
- Controlling
- Self-criticism
- Discipline

can avoid guilt or self-criticism. Therefore, a Core Belief Profile One's anger is typically focused on violations of standards.

Since the Core Belief Profile One is focused on being and doing the right thing they will react to what they perceive as being wrong. Their focus is on being right, particularly compared to other people, which gives them a sense that they are better than others. When a Core Belief Profile One walks into a room, they may subconsciously think, 'This place is so sloppy and disorganised. If I were in charge, things would not be such a mess.' Because they are seeking approval for having done the right thing, anything that is perceived to be wrong will represent an irritant that MUST be removed.

Further, their focus on creating order will bring anything that is out of order into stark relief. Once the source of chaos is removed or corrected, then all will be right and they can feel affirmed or secure.

## At work

### The dos and don'ts of working with Ones

- Do be neat. It counts for a great deal. This applies to both your person and your messages to the CBP One. They confuse the medium with the message or messenger.
- Do express yourself politely and with consideration. CBP Ones believe in etiquette, so use socially polite words such as: 'please', 'thank you', and 'you are welcome'.
- Do be punctual. CBP Ones are fixated on staying on schedule. If you make them late they are unlikely to quickly forgive or forget.
- Don't try to subvert the proper channels. They exist for the purpose of maintaining order and so must be adhered to.
- Do admit your mistakes and genuinely apologise. Don't make generalisations. Be very, very specific about what you admit to doing wrong.
- Do play according to the organisation's rules. If you are in charge, explain how you want something done. If your superior is a CBP One, find the exact way they want it done and then do it that way.
- Don't disagree with a CBP One. Instead, present your argument in a 'what if' fashion.
- Do anticipate the problems in your own area of concern. A CBP

One will discount your contribution if you are not perceived as being able to find the likely problems in your own area of responsibility.

- Don't offer criticism without providing a consistent objective framework for the criticism. CBP Ones will want to know what rules they have violated – and they will want a copy of the rule book.

*(Adapted from Goldberg, 1999, pp6,7)*

## Managing yourself as a One

- Try to model the behaviour that you want to see in others. Do not merely criticise others until they comply with your expectations.
- Appreciate that many of your comments will be taken as criticism, regardless of whether you see them that way.
- Consider the context of any criticism. While it may be appropriate for a specific behaviour, your context may be skewed and may ignore a great deal of relevant information.
- Aspire to your idealism but do not hold yourself and others to attaining it in every area of life.
- Develop realistic expectations for yourself.
- Appreciate and accept that making mistakes is part of the learning process.
- Learn when the given time would be better prioritised on other tasks rather than transforming a workable job to a perfect job.
- Understand that people do not want to be judged. So if you insist on constantly offering criticism you will be shunned and avoided. This will seriously limit your career development.
- Do not adopt the position of moral champion; take a break from the job of policing everyone around you.
- You probably have a tendency to accept and comply blindly with the rules of other people and institutions. You need to develop your own principles and practices based on context.

*(Adapted from Goldberg, 1999, pp47–48)*

## As a customer

The CBP One has a very specific focus when they are purchasing goods or services. The CBP One will want to make purchases that are thrifty, but that are also premium quality for money. They view purchases as a form of investment for the family and so they require careful consideration in order to reach the right decision. The CBP One desires to have highly reliable goods or services that represent value for money.

## At home

### As a partner

The CBP One can be stingy with what they own and what they earn. They can become personally isolated by the belief that individuals do not willingly share what they have. Affection, love and support must be earned through good behaviour. Any failure to adhere to a rigid system of personal improvement indicates questionable moral character. Whatever the CBP One disapproves of in themselves will become the focal point of their criticism of others. The CBP One will not allow themselves to express 'inappropriate' emotions. As a consequence they have a deep-rooted fear of becoming out of control and their suppressed feelings become magnified in importance. Furthermore, this constant suppression of 'negative' emotions results in a significant sacrifice of emotional information (Palmer, 1995).

### Dos and don'ts

- Do remember the details. CBP Ones are very detail-conscious and so they will appreciate small gestures like being on time or remembering names.
- Do talk in a respectful manner. Ensure that no one appears stupid and ask for permission.
- Do praise their efforts and dependability as well as their thrift.
- Don't expect compliments in return.
- Do establish a program for personal development. Set improvement goals.
- Don't boast about your achievements or improvements.
- Do admit to mistakes or errors straight away. This will avoid a build-up of resentment.

- Do establish mutual responsibilities and requirements. This helps lessen the CBP One's sense that either of you might not be doing the right things in the relationship.
- Don't let your relationship become a power struggle. Ones need to be right. Look for other right answers.
- Do use humour to gently help them laugh at themselves. Use fun and novelty in relating.
- Do develop your own interests since Ones are tireless workers.

*(Adapted from Palmer, 1995, pp48–49)*

## As a child

As children, the CBP Ones remember being punished for bad or impulsive behaviour. They learned that to control impulsive behaviour, especially expressions of anger, would please their parents. CBP Ones believed that such control could make them appear good boys or good girls in the eyes of their parents. Therefore, the child sought to be affirmed and commended for being good, correcting error and meeting the demands of their critical mind. As a child, the CBP One came to the conclusion that people are not accepted for who they are but for their behaviour. Any behaviour, thought or emotion that is judged inappropriate is bad and should be punished within themselves and within others. For example, in the eyes of a child, anger seems to rise to almost murderous proportions and so no expression of anger is possible (Palmer, 1988).

# CBP One at their worst

At their worst the CBP One is a hyper-critical, self-righteous individual fixated on adhering to the rules regardless of the situation or circumstance. They can be incapable of giving praise or appreciation for anything or anyone – since nothing ever reaches perfection. At their worst the greatest compliment that a CBP One can give is, 'There was nothing that I could criticise in the work that you did.'

## Case study

Robert Greene (1998, pp393–394) tells the story of Oliver Cromwell who was absolutely certain of what needed to be done. He was determined to break up the power and wealth of the Catholic Church, making way for the Protestant Church, in as short a time as possible. While his certainty may have been seen as religious faith and fervour, it actually came from his chemical disposition, causality consciousness. Since his decision was chemically driven, he ignored the fact that his speedy reforms would cause pain and resentment. He calculated that these feelings would fade away quickly.

In 1534 Oliver Cromwell was given the position of being the king's secretary. This was due to his support of King Henry VIII of England when he was determined to separate his throne from the Roman Catholic Church. In that very same year Cromwell laid the foundation of his program of religious conversion by undertaking a complete survey of the churches and monasteries of England and of the wealth that they had accumulated over the centuries. The result was far more riches than he had imagined.

To justify his plans, Cromwell circulated stories about the corruption in the English monasteries, their abuse of power and their exploitation of the people they supposedly served. These rumours supported his self-justifying reframe of being absolutely certain of the right way to go. He started seizing the holdings of each monastery and dismantling it, with the Parliament's support.

While he was doing this, he also began to impose Protestantism on the people of England. He did this by introducing reforms in religious ritual and punishing those who remained with the Catholic process. The latter he labelled heretics. 'Wrapped in his self-righteousness, he failed to appreciate how horrified Britons were as churches were demolished, images of the Madonna and saints were broken in pieces, stained-glass windows were smashed, and the churches' treasures were confiscated. Without the monasteries, which had previously supported the poor, these people started flooding onto the streets. As further indication of his intolerance, Cromwell levied high taxes to pay for his ecclesiastical reforms, so certain was he that he knew the 'right way to go.' (Greene, pp393–394)

In June of 1540, Cromwell was arrested on charges that he was a Protestant extremist and a heretic. As a consequence he was sent to the Tower of London and was executed within six weeks. There was a very large and enthusiastic crowd who watched his execution.

## Exemplars of the type

| | |
|---|---|
| Hillary Clinton | Queen Elizabeth II |
| Malcolm Fraser | Cate Blanchett |
| Harrison Ford | George Harrison |
| General Colin Powell | Al Gore |
| Fred Nile | Martha Stewart |
| Peter Garrett | Mahatma Gandhi |
| Andrew Lloyd Webber | Bono |
| Helen Clark | Katherine Hepburn |

# Core Belief Profile Two – Helpers

The Core Belief Profile Two has a strong need to be perceived as a loving person and so their focus of attention goes to meeting the needs and desires of other people. They are constantly thinking, 'Will I be liked?' Since they focus on achieving a 'Yes' answer, they will seek to develop a deep emotional connection to satisfy their needs for love and affection. They focus on the approval of others by meeting their needs and becoming indispensable to them.

Core Belief Profile Twos are adept at manoeuvring other people into liking them. They live with an assumption that almost anyone or anything can become available to them with the right approach or the proper amount of subtly applied special attention. They are a compliant profile as they suppress their own desires to focus on the needs of others. Their own needs become subordinated to the needs of others. They seek to earn the respect they crave.

## Emotional state

The Core Belief Profile Two is formed around the emotion of pride. In relationships pride manifests through being the favourite, the trusted confidant of the person they are in relationship with. This is pride because they become attractive by adjusting their personal focus and taking on their partner's interests, tastes and preferences. This gives them pride in feeling indispensable and at being important to the success of others. Pride expresses itself socially through having an ambitious social position and public image becomes crucial.

To the Core Belief Profile Two, other people appear very needy and they take a great deal of pride in meeting the needs of others. Frequently, the Core Belief Profile Two has repressed his or her own needs and has projected them onto others. Therefore, they will be especially attracted to either inspiring or powerful people (all the better to meet their personal needs), or to those in obvious need (so their value is more obvious).

When a Core Belief Profile Two walks into a room, they tend to subconsciously think, 'These poor people! I wish I had time to give everyone my attention. They look troubled – they need my help!' By approaching others from a position of being the loving person who

# Principal Characteristics – Profile Two

## Focus of attention

- The needs and wants of others, especially of people they care about and would like to have care about them
- Relationships
- The moment-to-moment feelings and emotions of others

(Adapted from Daniels, et. al. 2000, p26)

## Focus of energy

- Sensing the emotional needs of others and doing what pleases them
- Feeling good about being able to meet others' needs so well
- Creating good feelings in others
- Maintaining others' acceptance and approval
- Romantic attachment

(Quoted from Daniels, et. al. 2000, p26)

## Focus of avoidance

- Disappointing others
- Feeling rejected or unappreciated
- Dependence on others

(Quoted from Daniels, et. al. 2000, p26)

## Self-justifying reframes

- Being helpful and giving
- Being generous
- Sensitivity to the feelings of others
- Being supportive, appreciative and romantic
- High energy, exuberance and expressiveness

## Weakness

- Pride
- Flattery

## Preferred communication style

- Personal support allows them to relax and be more open to learning
- Since there is a fear of appearing foolish, may be hesitant to take initial risks
- May need extensive preparation and/or partnership in trying new things
- Important to feel personal rapport with the instructor/manager and it is important that the instructor/manager treats people in a caring way
- Clarity of content or retention of material may suffer from overemphasis on relating
- Capacity to adapt to new environments and new people supports the learning process

## Key words and traits

- Pride
- Love need
- Hedonism
- Seductiveness
- Assertiveness
- Nurturance and False Abundance
- Histrionics
- Impressionable
- Emotional

## Other Names for this Type

- Givers

gives their concern and service to others, Core Belief Profile Twos have a sense of being better than others.

Since they tend to repress their own desires to better satisfy the needs of others, they become highly dependent on other people to meet their repressed desires.

Any threat to their relationships, or any perceived depreciation of important connections, causes the Core Belief Profile Two considerable stress.

## At work

### The dos and don'ts of working with Twos

- Do provide a great deal of personal contact – face to face is best.
- Do be generous with your praise, approval and affection. They crave genuine admiration for their people skills and what they perceive as their own generosity. Imply that they have really satisfied your needs.
- A Two needs unending praise and they become vindictive when what they feel is owed them is withheld.
- Don't embarrass them as they dread humiliation.
- Do tell them your own real needs in a matter-of-fact way. Twos respond well to need as their need is to help others.
- Do be personal in your interactions with them, letting them know their personal effort is important to you.
- Do let them meet your needs as far as you feel comfortable. They will not expect you to return the favour, since their focus is on your needs.
- Don't try to bully or lead a Two, as they will become vindictive.
- Do find ways to help them expand their sphere of influence.
- Don't try to reduce their socialising. That is how they energise themselves and get their work done.

*(Adapted from Goldberg, 1999, pp78–79)*

## Managing yourself as a Two

- Turn your compassion onto yourself. Ask yourself, 'What are my real needs? Who really matters to me?' Take time to find out your own feelings, interests and desires.
- Allow people to, sometimes, solve their own problems. Be aware of your tendency to rescue others. Be clear about your roles and responsibilities.
- Appreciate that everyone else is not going to focus on meeting your needs. So have the courage to ask for what you want.
- Ensure that you are performing the content component of your work as well as the interpersonal side.
- Learn to be interdependent rather than dependent. Be realistic in seeing your importance and learn to simply ask for what you want.
- Learn to accept praise without discounting it.
- Learn to deal straight without manipulating.

*(Adapted from Goldberg, 1999, pp77, 78)*

## As a customer

The CBP Two wants to have a relationship with the person from whom they are purchasing. They will want to feel that they are being treated favourably as a sign that they have a special relationship with the person selling them the goods or services. The CBP Two will also frequently purchase little gifts for themselves just because they deserve it. These gifts will be small impulse purchases made to satisfy a fleeting fancy and justified due to all the efforts that they are making on behalf of others.

## At home

### As a partner

The CBP Two looks to other people – their wants, their potentials and what it is that they need. Desiring approval, the CBP Two will form an association in which they become indispensable and the other party feels flattered and chosen for special recognition. Relationships then depend on what CBP Twos will or will not give. For the CBP Two, their partner's needs scream loudly and so the Two will respond by adapting themselves to please the other, being highly supportive and having pride in being of help.

The CBP Two seeks to be attractive by adjusting their focus, taking on a partner's interests and sharing their tastes. They have a talent for making people feel good about themselves and can please very difficult people.

Frequently a CBP Two will feel that they have many different selves, each matching the needs and desires of a specific relationship (Palmer, 1995).

## Dos and don'ts

- Do understand that they want to be the central figure in their life. They want to feel that they do not need you, but you need them.
- Do learn to recognise their manipulative techniques, complaints and use of guilt.
- Do be sensitive to the CBP Two's probable inexperience with intimacy. Rather than mutuality they have always tried to be and act as they think will please others. They need to know you will love them whether or not they meet all your needs.
- Do appreciate how they control while appearing to bend and yield.
- Do anticipate large emotional swings. The signals of unmet needs are anger and hysteria. While they may not recognise that they need something, they will become hysterical if they do not get it.
- Do encourage the CBP Two to be authentic.
- Do realise that sex or demonstrations of affection are equivalent to love for a CBP Two.
- Don't be surprised when the CBP Two begins to fight for freedom as they start to feel sold out by their habit of pleasing others, including you.
- Do realise that CBP Twos like relationships with problems. Then they can focus on the problem rather than the growth needed for two-way intimacy.

*(Adapted from Palmer, 1995, pp72–73)*

## As a child

As children they usually experienced a deep love and attention from one or both of their parents. In order to continue the flow of this love, the CBP Two developed the habit of anticipating the needs and desires of powerful others in their life and also of presenting themselves as being helpful and giving.

Another scenario may have been that a parent had significant physical and emotional needs that were met by the child. As a consequence, the child sought to have his or her own needs for love and affirmation met by meeting those of powerful others.

The world view that they adopted was that their needs could only be met through the agency of powerful others. Their survival strategy is to please others and to protect their sensitive connections to powerful agencies (Palmer, 1988).

## CBP Two at their worst

When the emotion of pride becomes all consuming then the CBP Two not only avoids their own needs but ceases to be aware that they have any needs at all. The CBP Two is more easily able to recognise the needs of their spouse, family or of the person they are with rather than see their own. This often involves them in transferring their own needs onto other people. For example, if a CBP Two were cold, they may ask someone else, 'Are you cold?' rather than recognising that they themselves are cold. This creates a manipulative tendency where the CBP Two uses the feelings and needs of others to get their own needs fulfilled. Another downside of this tendency is that frequently the help that the CBP Two offers is not the help that is desired or required.

### Case study

Greene (1998, pp137–140) tells about Muhammad, who was driven by Core Belief Profile Two. A massive empire was founded in the early part of the thirteenth century by Muhammad, the Shah of Khwarem. This empire had as its capital Samarkand, incorporating modern Turkey and parts of Afghanistan. The Shah formed a powerful and well-trained army, and his fighting forces could number 200,000 warriors within days. But his temporal powers eventually led to his downfall.

After he had consolidated his power Muhammad received an emissary from a new tribal leader to the east, Genghis Khan, in 1219. Khan gave Muhammad many gifts representing the finest goods from his small but quickly growing Mongol Empire. It was the desire of Genghis Khan to reopen the Silk Route to Europe and he suggested that this could be shared with Muhammad, along with a promise of peace between the two empires.

In his pride, Muhammad refused to acknowledge the man he saw as an upstart from the east, who, it seemed to him, was extremely arrogant to try to talk as an equal to one so clearly his superior. Muhammad completely ignored Khan's offer. So Genghis attempted diplomacy once again. On this occasion he sent a caravan with over one hundred camels filled with the most costly possessions garnered from his plunder of China. Before the caravan reached Muhammad, Inalchik, the governor of a nearby region, killed the leaders and took the booty.

Genghis Khan was sure that this must have been some sort of mistake and that Inalchik must have acted without Muhammad's direction. So the long-suffering Genghis Khan sent yet another mission to Muhammad. This time he reiterated his offer and asked that the governor be punished.

Refusing to see his own need for peace, Muhammad himself had one of the ambassadors executed and the other two had their heads shaved, a terrible insult to a Mongol warrior.

Having failed at diplomacy, Khan sent a message to Muhammad: 'You have chosen war. What will happen will happen, and what it is to be we know not; only God knows.' (Greene, 1998, p139). In 1220 he attacked Inlachik's province and quickly seized the capital where he executed the captured governor by having molten silver poured into his eyes and ears.

In the course of the next few years, Genghis Khan was able to utterly defeat Muhammad's army, surround Samarkand and then seize it.

Muhammad fled, and a year later died, his vast empire broken and destroyed. Genghis Khan was sole master of Samarkand, the Silk Route and most of northern Asia because of Muhammad's pride that refused to recognise his own need for peace.

## Exemplars of the type

| | |
|---|---|
| Blanche D'Alpuget | Lady Fairfax |
| Kofi Annan | Leo Schofield |
| Oprah Winfrey | Marilyn Monroe |
| John Travolta | Ros Packer |
| Angelina Jolie | Mother Teresa |
| Kate Fisher | Desmond Tutu |

# Core Belief Profile Three – Achievers

The Core Belief Profile Three desires to be seen as a successful person and so they tend to focus on achievement, on image and on what they produce.

They seek to be seen as successful through a single-minded pursuit of an objective, through hard work, efficiency and competition. Looking good and the image of appearing successful are as important as success itself.

They are focused on high-profile achievement and will avoid failing at all costs.

The Core Belief Profile Three assumes that people receive love and approval by achieving success, and they are rewarded by what they do and what they are perceived to have. Therefore, they are highly motivated and energetic at achieving their goals, and they constantly focus on the work that needs to be done. Their own positive self-esteem is based on personal productivity and winning. The Core Belief Profile Three is an assertive profile in that it demands the attention and respect that it craves in social settings.

## Emotional state

The Core Belief Profile Three is formed around the emotional state of deceit. This involves maintaining an image of success in the eyes of others, and this image is more important than substance. The image of being a successful person can be tailored to suit what is most successful in different situations.

Since they are always changing themselves to be consistent with the most successful image of whatever group or individual they are participating with, they deceive themselves and others. This can be expressed as 'just putting a little spin on the facts' or using charm and self-promotion.

The Core Belief Profile Three is an assertive profile because it moves against others and, in the face of stress, will expand his or her sense of self.

As far as possible, Core Belief Profile Threes will find subtle ways to get positive regard from others so they will feel like the centre of the room,

# Principal Characteristics – Profile Three

## Focus of attention

- Things to be done: tasks, goals and future achievements
- The most efficient solution
- How to be the best

(Adapted from Daniels, et. al. 2000, p 30)

## Focus of energy

- Doing things quickly and efficiently
- Staying active and busy
- Competing
- Gaining recognition and credit for achievements
- Adjusting to whatever is required for success
- Promoting themselves
- Looking good

(Adapted from Daniels, et. al. 2000, p 30)

## Focus of avoidance

- Failing to achieve their desired goals
- Being overshadowed by others
- Losing face
- Uncomfortable feelings and doubts that arise from inactivity and slowing their pace
- Whatever distracts them from getting things done, including emotions

(Adapted from Daniels, et. al. 2000, p 30)

## Self-justifying reframes

- Being personable
- Enthusiasm
- Leadership
- Self-assurance
- Being practical, competent and efficient

- Inspiring hope
- Poise

## Weaknesses

- Vanity
- Deceit

## Preferred communication style

- Prefer fast-paced, clear, and challenging communication process
- Usually looking forward to the application of new material
- Wants the manager to be competent and successful
- Biased in favour of action; doesn't have to understand everything at the outset; willing to take results as they come
- Tendency to wing it
- Convergent thinking: all possibilities and elements are focused towards a single goal

## Key words and traits

- Attention
- Need and vanity
- Success through appearances
- Social sophistication and skill
- Cultivation of sexual attractiveness
- Other directedness
- Pragmatism
- Active vigilance
- Superficiality

as if to say, 'Look at what I have achieved. Look at me and affirm my value.' The feeling is that anything meaningful that occurs in a social setting occurs because of them.

## At work

### The dos and don'ts of working with Threes

- Do come straight to the point.
- Do ensure that you are scheduled onto their list. They will be busy and so will need to include you amongst their things to get done.
- Don't waste a CBP Three's time. Therefore, be prepared and well organised for any meeting.
- Don't interrupt a CBP Three when they are engaged in an activity.
- Do deliver on what you promise. Since the Three is committed, you should be as well. Doing is the area where Threes are most comfortable; so you must prove yourself in the area of their greatest concern.
- Do establish clear parameters that define success. Be explicit about what is expected to be achieved and how performance will be measured.
- Do provide very clear and well defined feedback so that the CBP Three knows what is required and that their efforts are being noticed and acknowledged.
- Do provide short-range plans and deadlines or at least reasonable points that will provide feedback. CBP Threes despise unclear expectations or responsibilities that do not have discernible boundaries.
- Don't compete with a Three. Instead, collaborate for success together.
- Don't expect to receive emotional encouragement from a Three for a job well done. A well done job is the standard and need not be praised.

*(Adapted from Goldberg, 1999, p 110)*

## Managing yourself as a Three

- Recognise that success is not proof of virtue.
- Recognise that there is a difference between who you are and what you do and learn to value both independently.
- Note your automatic tendency to take over, whether it is a good idea or not. Allow others to lead and see where they go.
- Take time in your schedule for other people – without an agenda or need for results!
- Develop the ability to be honest about how you feel.
- Develop the capacity to make a personal connection with those around you.

*(Adapted from Goldman, 1999, p 111)*

## As a customer

The CBP Three will make purchases with an eye towards efficiency. The efficiency that they are looking for is, given the amount of money that they have to spend, how can they make it stretch so they look their best. They will be constantly looking for goods or services that help them appear successful and they will want as many of these as they can afford. As a result they will look to use discounts or special rates whenever possible. This means they will be very interested in imitations of high quality products and they will use coupons or discount cards. They will want to appear successful in whatever purchase they make. Something of low quality that imitates success is far better than something that is high quality that does not scream prestige – particularly if it is cheaper!

## At home

### As a partner

In relationships, the CBP Three becomes the prototype of what their mate finds attractive. They become the ideal lover or the attentive mate. Their emphasis is on form and surface. They can adopt the role model of whatever it is that their partner finds appealing, and in the process they deceive themselves that their appropriate feelings are actually genuine feelings.

This CBP has a tendency to view feelings as something to do. This involves seeing how others react and then pretending to have those feelings when they become appropriate. At times when, say, the emotion of love is called for then the CBP Three will adopt the facial expressions and body postures of love while their mind continues to focus on a list of things that requires doing. Since they expect to be loved for performance, the CBP Three will try very hard to do whatever the relationship requires. Unfortunately, this will be a lie with no source of truth whatsoever (Palmer, 1995).

## Dos and don'ts

- Do remember that CBP Threes will feel loved for their achievements and not for who they are.
- Do bear in mind that they frame the relationship in terms of activity to be accomplished. Therefore, they may show affection and feelings according to an ideal script. Help them to slow down their intimate activity and feel the feelings.
- Do remember that they require praise for their winning image and style.
- Do appreciate that a CBP Three will feel threatened when real emotions rise to the surface. They will need to be reassured that they are in fact doing (or feeling) the right thing.
- When the CBP Three takes responsibility for the negative emotions of other people, do help them appreciate that there is no quick solution to pain.
- Do let them know that you appreciate them for who they are and not purely for what it is that they do.
- Do strongly encourage them to take breaks from work, which is their main focus in life.

*(Adapted from Palmer, 1995, pp 94-5)*

## As a child

As children, CBP Threes were generally affirmed and loved for what they achieved and what they produced rather than for who they were as a person. They came to the conclusion that projecting the image of success and achievement would attain recognition and praise. Therefore, they learned to cultivate an image of success, high performance, efficiency and hard work to ensure affirmation and love (Palmer, 1988).

## CBP Three at their worst

The deceit of the CBP Three that is most easily seen is self-deceit. However, it is also the deception of others. Since the CBP Three is constantly changing themselves to be consistent with the most successful image of whatever group or individual they are participating with, they deceive themselves and others that they are actually what it is that they are doing. This deceit can manifest itself as simply putting one's best foot forward by just placing a little spin on the facts to sound good, charm or to self-promote. Deceit is a desire for approval measured by material success.

### Case study

Another story told by Greene (1998, pp37–58) is of Thomas Edison, a prime example of Core Belief Profile Three. Much of Edison's fame was generated from the work and brains of others. A prime example of how he stole the spotlight from others was in relation to the Serbian scientist Nikola Tesla. As a young man, hired by Edison, Tesla worked like a slave to perfect Edison's model. Tesla eventually offered to redesign the dynamos completely. Edison was certain this could not be done, at least in the short term. He did not share these thoughts with Tesla, rather, he offered him fifty thousand dollars upon completion.

Nikola Tesla worked even harder than before and after only a year he had radically improved the dynamos to a fully automated version. While Edison was very pleased with the improvements, he broke his promise, telling the young Serb, "Tesla, you do not understand our American humour!' (Greene, 1998, p57). Instead of the money, Edison offered him a small raise. But Edison was very pleased with the improvements and proceeded to take all the credit.

Tesla passionately pursued the creation of an alternative-current system (AC) for electricity. Thomas Edison felt that the existing direct current system (DC) was all that was needed and so he not only refused to support Tesla's research but also tried to sabotage his work. When Tesla appeared to have succeeded in creating an AC system, Edison was furious and set out to try and ruin Tesla's reputation and discredit the AC system. He made it appear inherently unsafe and claimed that Tesla was irresponsible for promoting it.

It is known that to do this Thomas Edison captured all kinds of pets and proceeded to electrocute them with an AC current. When this wasn't enough, in 1890 he arranged for New York State prison authorities to organise the world's first execution by electrocution, using an AC current.

Unfortunately, all of Edison's experiments had been conducted on small creatures and so the charge used on the man was too weak, and he was subjected to extreme pain rather than death. The prisoner had to be executed in a different way. It was a dreadful event and almost ruined Edison's reputation.

On another occasion, Edison was offered the Nobel Prize for his inventions. When he found that he would need to share the prize and the spotlight with Tesla he said, "I would rather no prize, than to share a prize with him!" And so his need to be the centre of attention made him turn down the Nobel Prize.

Edison once stated that 'he did not need to be a mathematician since he could always hire one.' (Greene, 1998, p58). He was skilful at being a businessman and at being a publicist but not as an inventor or scientist. His fame came from his ability to promote his business and use the ideas of others.

## Exemplars of the type

- Kieren Perkins
- Michael Jordan
- Shane Warne
- Arnold Schwarzenegger
- Peter Costello
- Kevin Rudd
- Nicole Kidman
- Paris Hilton
- Bob Hawke
- Elle McPherson
- Sharon Stone
- Brad Pitt
- Tom Cruise
- Peter Beattie
- David Beckham
- Lisa McCune
- Malcolm Turnbull

# Core Belief Profile Four – Artists

The Core Belief Profile Four is a unique person and focuses on being special and distinctive. They are absorbed in an emotional world, so emotional connection and relationships are important to the Fours and they value highly the expression of authentic feelings. The Core Belief Profile Four focuses on living a unique and extraordinary life and they tend to long for the unobtainable, whatever that may be.

The reason that Core Belief Profile Fours are drawn to deep connections is that they feel they need to keep searching for an ideal love or for perfect circumstances to make them complete. The underlying assumption is that there is more to life than merely the ordinary. This means that they will be sensitive to emotions and feelings in others and will experience intense feelings from great joy to depression. The Core Belief Profile Fours are a socially withdrawn profile because they tend to hide themselves in the hope that someone will discover and appreciate their uniqueness. While they want attention, they withdraw from social settings with the hope that someone will seek them out and appreciate them for being the unique creature that they feel themselves to be.

## Emotional state

The Core Belief Profile Four is formed around the emotion of envy because they feel they have been denied the feelings of contentment and fulfilment that other people appear to experience. This envy fuels a search for the objects and status that supposedly make people satisfied. It also creates a cycle of desire, acquisition, disappointment and rejection as the Core Belief Profile Four pulls for the unobtainable and pushes away when it comes within reach. This envy will arise in comparison to others, in competition with people for approval or through rivalry with those who claim the recognition that they want.

The Core Belief Profile Four is focused on being unique and special and responds to stress by moving away from engagement with the world and into an inner space in their imagination. Their focus is on what is not in their lives: people who have disappointed them, let them down or left them; and on being slighted, rejected or abandoned. When a Core Belief Profile Four enters a room, their sense of self is 'I am not part of what is going on. I am not like these other people. I do not fit in.' They will then reinforce this position by being standoffish and aloof and

# Principal Characteristics – Profile Four

## Focus of attention

- What is positive and attractive about the future and the past
- What is missing or distant that they long for and feel lonely without
- What is aesthetically pleasing and deeply touching or meaningful

(Adapted from Daniels, et. al. 2000, p 34)

## Focus of energy

- Intense feelings of sadness and longing associated with what seems to be missing or lacking in their life
- Finding love, meaning and fulfilment through self-expression and deep connection
- Creating themselves to be unique individuals

(Adapted from Daniels, et. al. 2000, p 34)

## Focus of avoidance

- Being rejected, abandoned, not heard, or insignificant
- Feeling they do not measure up
- Feeling there is something wrong with them
- The mundane
- People and experiences that lack emotional depth

(Adapted from Daniels, et. al. 2000, p 34)

## Self-justifying reframes

- Sensitivity
- A creative orientation
- Being attuned to feelings
- A capacity to empathise with suffering
- Intensity, passion
- Romantic idealism

- Emotional depth
- Authenticity
- Introspection

## Weaknesses

- Envy
- Longing
- Melancholy

## Preferred communication style

- Responses to material can change based on inner feeling state
- Prefers experiential training, which is useful for achieving personal involvement
- Material should be 'attractive' in order to bring out internal experience and engagement with others
- Affinity for metaphor and symbols leading to deeper meanings
- Needs to understand the theory and the 'why' of things
- Wants personal rapport with the instructor/manager
- In performance or test situations can lose focus even though competent or knowledgeable

## Key words and traits

- Envy
- Poor self-image
- Focus on suffering
- Nurturance
- Emotionality
- Competitive arrogance
- Refinement
- Artistic interests

## Other Names for this Type

- Elitist, Romantic

acting in a mysterious fashion.

# At work

## The dos and don'ts of working with Fours

- Do allow the Four to develop the end result. Provide them with a process, not just a rigid goal. Say, 'Paint me a picture' or 'Tell me the story,' not 'Just the facts please,' to allow the Four to communicate important material.
- Don't try and use material incentives for a Four to abandon their goal. This will go nowhere.
- Do go out of your way to praise the Four for their unique perspective and insight. While they may not need your help to feel special, they like being recognised for their uniqueness. If you want them to work hard and well, detail how a project requires their personal touch and how without their input it will fail.
- Don't minimise their feelings. This only makes them wrap themselves more tightly about their feelings.
- Don't presume that you know what will satisfy them. They must find their own motivation; all you can do is accept whatever this is.
- Do try to empathise with them rather than attempting to assist them.
- Don't try to give them an answer to their quandaries. Instead, let them express themselves for however long this takes.
- Don't ask a Four to lower their intensity. They equate this with being dishonest. A much better approach is to get them to widen their approach to include additional factors and information.
- Do ensure that you communicate that their creative ideas have been received, understood and appreciated. This is everything to them.
- Do provide assurances of your commitment to them. A Four will consistently be on the lookout for the possibility of abandonment. Don't give them reason to feel abandoned.

*(Adapted from Goldberg, 1999, p 138)*

## Managing yourself as a Four

- Do not give up. While despair shadows you, fight to see that everything is not actually a lost cause.
- Your feelings need not determine everything that you do. Learn to name them rather than just to be them. Convey emotions rather than being forced to act them out.
- Do not stew in your emotions if you can help it. Move your body instead – depression is linked to energy flow and movement is an appropriate means of changing it.
- Question yourself if you are ignoring a colleague's contribution because you have judged them as shallow.
- Do not confuse compromise with appropriate negotiations. The ability to collaborate and to factor in practical considerations can make your projects stronger.
- Not everything is completely personal.

## As a customer

The CBP Four will make purchases that reinforce their own unique and special nature. Purchases that are somehow completely different or unreplicable will attract them. They will make self-indulgent purchases – to make up for the fact that no one seems to appreciate their uniqueness. What they buy will reflect their own emotional journey.

## At home

### As a partner

When a CBP Four feels that their heart has been touched by someone they have an impulse to follow those feelings and to abandon caution in the pursuit of having their emotional needs met. This deep requirement makes ordinary relating difficult since they want absolute emotional presence from a partner. They desire unwavering devotion, and they are highly concerned with abandonment.

The typical pattern of the CBP Four in relating is their push-pull pattern of attraction. They absolutely must have someone when they want them, they adore them and they worship them. When they no longer want the individual, they reject them and become spiteful. The CBP Four distances themselves when others want them and then they start to crave attention and relationship when the partner begins to move away (Palmer, 1995, pp119–120).

## Dos and don'ts

- Do appreciate that the CBP Four will feel that there is something missing in their life. Other couples appear to be happier and more fulfilled.
- Do count on complex relating. Nothing is simple with them and so depth of relating, rather than fun, is the goal.
- Do come to expect impatience with the flatness of daily life and relationship. The daily experiences are intensified through sabotage, suffering and dramatic acts.
- It is always show time. Extravagant preparation is necessary to create a dramatic setting for relationships. Unique self-presentation compensates for the inner feelings of deprivation because romance is idealised and almost unattainable.
- Do realise that it is the pursuit and not the happiness that matters most to the CBP Four. They may feel melancholy, nostalgic, withdrawn, dramatic, passionate or intense in their seeking.
- Don't expect the CBP Four to appreciate present opportunities or experiences to the full. They spend much of their time reminiscing over the perfect love affair or desiring some future objective.
- Do appreciate the push-pull pattern of attention. When you are with them the CBP Four will see your negative aspects; when you are not present then they will see only your positive aspects. This contributes to their pervading sense of abandonment and loss.
- Do appreciate that they are sensitive to your emotions and will support you through your painful times.

*(Adapted from Palmer, 1995, pp118–119)*

## As a child

As children, the CBP Four experienced a deep personal loss or disconnection from a significant relationship. In the majority of instances, this would have been with the loss of parental love. This loss is a source of deep longing by the child who romanticises and idealises this unique relationship, while continually experiencing the melancholy of loss. Some CBP Fours report that as a result of a childhood sickness they were 'kept in cotton wool' and felt disconnected from relationships with their peers and siblings. As a result the child learnt to idealise and romanticise their relationships while longing for that ideal and unique relationship (Palmer, 1988).

## CBP Four at their worst

At their worst the CBP Four will be completely driven by their envy. This results in a constant awareness that others have what is missing in their own life since envy manifests as dissatisfaction with one's current status in comparison with others. Envy can also manifest as an awareness of what else there is in the world that the CBP Four would like or need. Often it is accompanied by a sense of personal flaws or lack. At their worst, the CBP Four will experience intense competition for approval and the symbols that represent it. This will be observed in their seeking attention through beauty, drama, creative acts, unique perspectives and wilful behaviour. It will also be accompanied by rapidly changing mood swings, bouts of self-pity and dramatic expressions of anger.

### Case study

Greene's story (Greene, 1998, pp55–79) which exemplifies this profile is of Marie Gilbert of Ireland who arrived in Paris in the 1840s in order to make her fortune as a dancer and performer. Changing her name to Lola Montez she asserted that she was a flamenco dancer from Spain. Unfortunately for Lola her career languished and by 1845, in order to survive, she became a courtesan and quickly became one of the more successful in Paris.

There was only one man with enough influence and power to save Lola's dancing career, Alexandre Dujarier, the owner and operator of the largest circulating newspaper in France. Giving in to her envy for what she did not have, Lola was determined to woo and conquer Alexandre. To this end she investigated his habits, discovering that he habitually rode every day. A horse rider herself, Lola contrived to ride with him. From then on they rode together and eventually shared the same apartment.

Their happiness was complete. But only for a while, since envy can never be satisfied. Lola Montez began to resurrect her dancing career, with the help of Dujarier. Dujarier claimed that he would marry her in the spring. However, he was completely unaware that Lola had eloped at age nineteen with an Englishman, and had not divorced. Dujarier's life started to fall apart. His business fortunes turned against him and he lost his friends.

Lola began to see things in a new light. She was used to being pampered and showered with gifts. Why should a special person like her live such a dull life with an ordinary man? On the night of their very first quarrel, Dujarier attended a party alone. There he insulted an influential drama critic, Jean-Baptiste Rosemond de Beauvallon. The very next morning Beauvallon, one of the best pistol shots in France, challenged Dujarier to a duel. While Dujarier attempted to apologise, Beauvallon refused to accept and Alexandre Dujarier was shot and killed.

In a state of high melancholy, Lola left Paris.

In 1846 Lola Montez arrived in Munich, where she was determined to conquer King Ludwig of Bavaria. Again her envy caused her to look for the most powerful individual who could supply her needs. She set about her investigations and soon found that the best way to Ludwig was through his aide-de-camp, Count Otto von Rechberg, a flirtatious man. On a day when the Count was having breakfast at an outdoor café, Lola rode by on her horse and was 'accidentally' thrown from the saddle at the feet of Rechberg. The Count offered his assistance to the distressed Lola and quickly became ensnared by her. Rechberg promised to set up Lola with Ludwig.

An audience was arranged between the King and Lola, but when she arrived to meet him she could hear the King saying he was far too busy to entertain a favour-seeking foreigner. Refusing to be denied her catch, Lola thrust aside the sentries barring the King's presence and brazenly entered the room. In the process the front of her dress 'somehow' became ripped and to the astonishment of all, Lola's bare breasts were blatantly exposed. The King granted her an audience. Fifty-five hours later Lola began her career in Bavaria; while the reviews were terrible, Ludwig was undeterred and arranged more performances.

Ludwig described himself as being 'bewitched' by Lola. And while he had a reputation for being a miser, and he was not given to flights of fancy, he soon began to bestow all manner of gifts onto Lola and started to write poetry about her. Having conquered the most powerful man in the country, Lola began to lose her sense of proportion and started to act in a manner that made the Bavarian commoners despise her.

The very Bavarians who had previously loved their King began to show signs of outward disrespect towards him. Regardless, Lola was given the title of Countess and she began to try her hand at politics, giving Ludwig advice on policy. Hers was the most powerful voice in the kingdom and she treated all the other ministers with complete contempt. Consequently, the once peaceful land erupted into riot. Bavaria was virtually in the grip of civil war and students everywhere were chanting 'Raus mit Lola!'– Get out Lola.

Ludwig was forced to order Lola to leave Bavaria in February of 1848. For more than five weeks the Bavarians poured out their wrath against their formerly admired King. By March, Ludwig was forced to abdicate.

Lola then moved to England. Seeking respectability she was determined to capture George Trafford Heald, who had an army career and influential parents. This was despite still being legally married. While George was more than ten years younger than Lola he quickly fell under her spell and they married in 1849. Unfortunately, Lola was soon arrested on charges of bigamy, since she still had not divorced her first young husband. Rather than face trial Lola skipped bail and fled with Heald to Spain. Their time together was tempestuous and they frequently quarrelled. On one occasion, Lola slashed George with a knife. In the end Lola thrust him away from her. This again indicates Lola's habit of creating drama for the sake of intensity, at someone else's expense. When George Heald came back to England he had no position in the army and was no longer welcome in society. So he moved to Portugal and lived in poverty until he died in a drunken boating accident.

Shortly after it was released, the man who published Lola Montez's autobiography filed for bankruptcy.

By 1853, Lola was living in California where she married a man named Pat Hull. Again she experienced a stormy relationship until she finally left Hull for someone else. Hull also ended up depressed and alcoholic, a condition which killed him four years later.

When she was forty one, Lola gave away all her clothes, finery and possessions and turned to God. She began to tour America as a lecturer on religious topics. She dressed all in white and wore a headgear that was like a halo. Lola Montez died two years after she began lecturing, in 1861.

## Exemplars of the type

- Madonna
- Elizabeth Taylor
- Liam Neeson
- Vincent Van Gogh
- James Dean
- Johnny Depp
- Sir Laurence Olivier
- Brett Whiteley
- Robert Hughes
- Patrick White
- Neil Young
- Edith Piaf
- Spencer Tracy
- Winona Ryder
- Princess Diana
- Alanis Morrisette
- Nora Jones

# Core Belief Profile Five – Analysts

The Core Belief Profile Five is the wise person who is highly observant and reflective. They use their observing and thinking as a way of ensuring an emotional separation from others and relationships. Core Belief Profile Fives tend to have a lifelong attachment to knowledge and value understanding highly. They have a special attraction to the secret and unexplained. They are described as maintaining an emotional distance from others, protecting their privacy, not getting involved, doing without and getting by on a minimum.

The reason that Core Belief Profile Fives withdraw into intellectualism is because they use this to protect themselves from intrusive demands and from being drained of their resources by becoming private and self-sufficient. The underlying assumption is that personal and physical resources are in short supply. Core Belief Profile Fives try to preserve their resources by becoming private and self-sufficient, while limiting their desires and accumulating a great deal of personal knowledge. The Core Belief Profile Five is a withdrawing profile in that it seeks security by withdrawing from people or situations that are perceived as threatening.

## Emotional state

The Core Belief Profile Five is formed around the emotion of avarice and a world view of general scarcity. Avarice manifests as a harbouring of resources – money, time, energy, food, the self or an attention to minimising waste. It is often accompanied by a sense of superiority in getting by with the least of something; for example, the least amount of money spent on food, or the smallest heating bill in the winter. This avarice is not just financial stinginess; it can also be a withholding of time, love or interest. Avarice is the state of having a desire to take everything in and an unwillingness to let anything go.

## At work

### The dos and don'ts of working with Fives

- Do provide the CBP Five with insider information. They love it. They want that special piece of knowledge that will provide them with extra insight. It is the mental equivalent to the Three's

# Principal Characteristics – Profile Five

## Focus of attention
- The intellectual domain
- Facts
- Analysis and compartmentalised thinking
- Intrusions or demands on them

(Adapted from Daniels, et. al. 2000, p38)

## Focus of energy
- Observing from a detached stance
- Learning all there is to know about a subject
- Thinking and analysing in advance
- Dampening and reducing feelings
- Self-containment, withdrawing, conserving
- Maintaining sufficient privacy, boundaries and limits

(Quoted from Daniels, et. al. 2000, p 38)

## Focus of avoidance
- Strong feelings, especially fear
- Intrusive or demanding people or circumstances
- Feelings of inadequacy and emptiness

(Quoted from Daniels, et. al. 2000, p 38)

## Self-justifying reframes
- Scholarliness
- Being knowledgeable
- Thoughtfulness
- Calmness in crisis
- Being respectful
- Keeping confidences
- Dependability
- Appreciation of simplicity

## Weaknesses
- Avarice
- Detachment

## Preferred communication style
- Prefers to maintain an observer role; doesn't want much direct attention or participation, especially at the beginning
- Attention moves to principles, concepts and systems. Researched content is favoured over anecdotal or hearsay content
- Likes to hear other people's experiences without a demand for personal contact
- Needs time to absorb and review new material
- May be listening well without showing much personal reaction

## Key words and traits
- Retentiveness
- Not giving
- Pathological detachment
- Fear of engulfment
- Autonomy
- Feeling nothing
- Postponement of action
- Guilt

## Other Names for this Type
- Observers, Investigators, Experts

competitive advantage.

- Include as much supporting data as you can since the Five will delight in the details. What you find as extremely trivial may be the central fact for a Five.
- Do appreciate that CBP Fives find meetings very difficult. Provide them with as much information before the meeting as you can: what is to be discussed, who will be there, what needs to be decided and what will be required of them. This final issue is the most crucial – they will want to know what it is that is required of them.
- Do allow, if it is at all feasible, the CBP Five to make decisions following the meeting, not during the meeting.
- Don't stray from the normal and agreed upon topics since the CBP Five may come to experience even normal questioning as cross examinations.
- Be direct, precise and concise and, most importantly, do not pry.
- Don't try to fill every space in the conversation.
- Do appreciate that a CBP Five absolutely requires privacy.
- Do make a private space when you are meeting with a CBP Five, particularly if it is about a sensitive issue. Shut the door and hold the phone calls. Create a safe, bounded physical and emotional space in which the two of you can interact.
- Don't try to get a reaction from them. This will not occur.
- Do allow a CBP Five to be, and feel, prepared for a meeting. Therefore give them plenty of advance warning about anything.

*(Adapted from Goldberg, 1999, pp170-171)*

## Managing yourself as a Five

- In work you must collaborate to succeed. Try to find production-oriented people so that you can bring your ideas to life.
- Look for feedback about the effect your communications are having on others. While it may feel that you are offering helpful ideas or facts, others may perceive you as being a condescending and arrogant know-it-all.
- Express your opinion! Other people are not mind-readers.
- Risk expressing your position first. Let other people align with your ideas.

- Don't always play it safe and hide. Consider that the decision to make your opinions and feelings known might not be the best way to go.
- Get out of the habit of thinking about what you are going to say while another person is talking. Instead, listen to what they are saying.
- Assess your plans to see if you have considered the human factor at all.
- If you ignore it, then your projects will be less than successful.
- Recognise that there is a difference between secrecy and privacy.
- While it is appropriate to keep a great deal of yourself private, there is no need to keep everything secret.
- Let your colleagues know that you are actually part of the team and that you support its objectives.
- Be generous with what you have. Whenever you are, you are effectively nourishing yourself.
- Try to monitor the message that others are taking from your silences.
- Do nothing to excess – including moderation! Learn to spend a little.

*(Adapted from Goldberg, 1999, pp171–172)*

## As a customer

The CBP Five will be a very objective purchaser. They will want to know all the information about different products and services and they will want to be able to compare in their own time without being pressured by a salesperson. They love internet sites that provide them with all the details about what they are considering purchasing. The key driver of the purchasing decision will be price. The CBP Five is very budget conscious.

## At home

### As a partner

Since the primary defence of the CBP Five is detachment, being in a relationship can seem dangerous to them. Disengaging thought from feeling is a habitual manner of operating. Life can seem to flow over you almost as though it never actually happened.

Making a commitment that lasts for years upsets private independence.

It is far easier to do without someone than to be in a position where they truly matter. They may well feel that emotional commitments are very demanding and that they need to withdraw and think about things. But they can be highly emotional when they are allowed freedom to express it in their own way.

They want emotional autonomy, so while you can be dependent and emotional, the CBP Five will not want to be drawn into those feelings (Palmer, 1995, pp139–141).

## Dos and don'ts

- Do understand that CBP Fives have delayed reactions and so their feelings can surface when they are alone. They can feel great tenderness as they reflect on the other.
- The CBP Five alternates between withdrawal and the desire to have someone break their isolation.
- Do appreciate that intimacy can stimulate detachment. They may convey the message that 'I have the capacity to go it alone' or that 'I don't actually need you.'
- Do realise that you may end up living in a compartmentalised aspect of the CBP Five's world, separated from the rest of it.
- If a CBP Five is emotionally attached, then they will become fiercely possessive of you since you are their emotional lifeline.

*(Adapted from Palmer, 1995, p139)*

## As a child

As children, CBP Fives report that they experienced psychic intrusions into their life by adults who demanded too much and returned far too little. These intrusions were such that the child closed down their emotions in self defence.

A second, less common scenario is that the child felt abandoned and so closed down in order to survive (Palmer, 1988). As a result, the child sought to protect itself from these intrusions and feelings of inadequacy through privacy, self-sufficiency, limiting desires and accumulating knowledge.

# CBP Five at their worst

When they are at their worst the CBP Five is driven by the belief that there is scarcity in the world, wastage and a limited amount of resources. They respond with avarice which manifests as a harbouring of resources, whatever they are: money, time, energy, food, the self or an attention to minimising waste. There is often a sense of superiority associated with getting by with the least amount of something: the least heat in winter, the least spent on food and so on. They can become dominated by the need to hoard resources, either to avoid being controlled by others or to be used as power over others. At their worst, the CBP Five will follow a period of being generous which is designed to create dependence, with periods of stinginess and withholding.

## Case study

Greene (1998, pp337–338) tells the tale of the Duke and Duchess of Marlborough who lived in the early eighteenth century and were highly esteemed by the English aristocracy of the day. The Duke, having succeeded against the French, was considered to be one of England's greatest generals. Queen Anne rewarded him after the battle of Blenheim with a plot of land and resources to build himself a great palace. The project was awarded to John Vanbrugh, a young and flamboyant architect and dramatist, who intended to design a magnificent monument to the owner's brilliance and power. It would include grand features such as seen in the most extravagant houses in Europe. Right from the start there was absolutely no way to please the Duchess. She thought that the architect was wasting money on needless embellishments; all she wanted was for the palace to be completed as soon as possible for as little money as possible. This shows avarice.

The Duchess proceeded to interrogate Vanbrugh and his workmen over absolutely every detail. She was obsessed with the pettiest of issues; even though the government was paying for the palace she insisted on counting absolutely every penny. She justified this behaviour by using the excuse that she was saving the family fortune. Eventually, her penny-pinching attitude and controlling behaviour caused the Queen to lose patience and dismiss her from the court. On exit, the Duchess, driven by her meanness, stripped the apartment of every frill and fixture, right down to the doorknobs.

As the project slowly progressed, she made life miserable for all the workmen who had to bear her abuse for every stone that was used. While the Duke only wanted to have his beautiful construction completed, his wife was so entrenched in meanness and control that the workers had to sue her to be paid. In the end the poor old man never got to sleep in his bed, as he died before his palace was finished. After the Duke's death, it was found that the obsession of the Duchess was unfounded. He had a large estate.

## Exemplars of the type

- Bill Gates
- Howard Hughes
- Kurt Cobain
- Stephen Hawking
- Albert Einstein
- Bernie Fraser
- John Le Carre
- Margaret Ollie
- Jane Goodall
- Laurie Anderson
- Jodie Foster

# Core Belief Profile Six – Loyal Sceptics

The Core Belief Profile Six is the loyal person in that they see themselves as being loyal, dutiful and doing what he or she ought to do. They seek relationships with others or with organisations that can protect them and to which they can respond with loyalty and duty. The Core Belief Profile Six focuses on gaining safety and avoiding harm through constant vigilance, questioning of motives and doubting.

The reason that they express loyalty and desire security is due to the assumption that the world is a dangerous place and that you simply cannot trust other people. Therefore, the focus of attention is on danger and potential threats that require constant vigilance and scanning of the environment to avoid. The Core Belief Profile Six is a compliant profile in that they try to obey the internalised rules, principles and dictates that they have learned from childhood. They try to earn the security that they are seeking.

## Emotional state

The emotion that dominates the Core Belief Profile Six is fear and it runs the gamut of flight to fight (or from phobic to counter-phobic). The flight form is referred to as a phobic Six, and they will be very aware of their fear and will avoid it. In contrast, the counter-phobic Six will directly attack the very thing that they fear the most, but they have no awareness of their fear. Both strategies are formed around the emotional state of fear. The Core Belief Profile Six spends a considerable amount of time preparing for the worst possible disasters, often thinking ahead to the worst-case scenarios and anticipating them. The need for absolute certainty frequently leads to endless planning and considerable procrastination from them.

The Core Belief Profile Six has a sense of being better than other people through their affiliations and social identifications. For example, 'I live in Sydney, which is better than Brisbane and so I am better than people who live in Brisbane.' Since they seek security, they want to earn this security through personal displays of loyalty and displays of the power of their affiliations.

# Principal Characteristics – Profile Six

### Focus of attention
- What could go wrong or be dangerous
- Potential pitfalls, difficulties, incongruities
- Implications, inferences, and hidden meanings

(Quoted from Daniels, et. al. 2000, p42)

### Focus of energy
- Doubting, testing and looking for double messages
- Logical analysis to figure things out
- Playing the devil's advocate
- Ambivalence towards authority
- Showing strength
- Gaining security by obtaining the goodwill of others, being loyal to others and dedicating themselves to worthy causes

(Adapted from Daniels, et. al. 2000, p42)

### Focus of avoidance
- Being helpless or not in control in the face of danger and harm
- Succumbing to danger or harm
- Getting stuck in doubt and contrary thinking
- Alienating people they depend on by contradicting or opposing them

(Adapted from Daniels, et. al. 2000, p42)

### Self-justifying reframes
- Trustworthiness
- Loyalty
- Thoughtfulness
- Questioning mind
- Warmth
- Perseverance
- Responsibility
- Protectiveness
- Intuition
- Wit
- Sensitivity

### Weaknesses
- Anxiety
- Doubt

### Preferred communication style
- Likes to compare and contrast; analytical
- Suspicious of the surface image, interested in the underlying content or meaning
- Wants to know the premise and bias of the manager; helped by clear statements of goals and intentions
- Prefers orientation and warm-up to build rapport, then willing to move quickly into content
- Doesn't want to be pushed; pacing is important; stops and starts are useful
- Modelling is important; doesn't want to jump immediately
- May challenge your authority; either directly or by deliberately making mistakes

### Key words and traits
- Fear
- Cowardice
- Anxiety
- Theoretical orientation
- Ingratiating friendliness
- Rigidity
- Pugnacity
- Orientation to authority and ideals

### Other Names for this Type
- Worriers

# At work

## The dos and don'ts of working with Sixes

- Do strive to keep your word. Nothing will help them more than their having a sense that you mean what you say, that you have integrity, and that you can be trusted.
- Do only commit to what you know you are capable of and then ensure that you keep all aspects of the commitment. They focus on explicit congruence between what you say and what you do.
- Don't expect to immediately earn trust. It will take awhile for them to feel that they can trust you. Let them. It is very important to them to see that you keep all your agreements – particularly the small ones.
- Don't engage in win-lose arguments with a CBP Six about something that they have their mind made up over. There is no way that you can change their opinion. It is better to expand the discussion to include alternative ideas and additional people.
- Don't exaggerate. Just tell the story straight. They have a terrifying fear of being conned in some way.
- Do make your allegiance clear. In their unconscious mind, the world is clearly split between the good (us) and the bad (them).
- Do disclose your self-interest as they like to know what is in it for you.
- Do intersperse the positives with negatives when you are communicating with them.
- Don't order a Six around. If you want a Six to do something, share your thought processes and give reasons.
- Do restate reality. Be aware that you will need to assist a Six's memory and reality check.
- Do establish a clear plan with fall-back positions. The Six does not like surprises. They want security and predictability.
- When the Six's considerations are out on the table, this is a good time for action. Acknowledge the mistakes that you make without taking blame for what is not your fault.
- Be straightforward about admitting when you are in trouble. Sixes understand trouble; after all, it is where they live.

*(Adapted from Goldberg, 1999, pp199–201)*

## Managing yourself as a Six

- Practise having confidence. When Sixes look for ways to trust others, they will find them.
- Some Sixes assume that their leader has all the answers and that they have none. They become completely compliant in order to avoid the constant doubting of no change authority. You must find your own inner sense of authority.
- Do not be afraid to play the role of devil's advocate. After all, it is what you do best anyway. You have developed formidable skill at cutting through pretence and exposing what will not work. Show where the problems and pitfalls are. Learn to give compliments; Sixes tend to have a problem with gratitude.
- Define your own positive goals and focus on them just as much as on where you can go wrong.
- To avoid constantly laying blame, focus on the problem and not on the person.

*(Adapted from Goldberg, 1999, p202)*

## As a customer

The CBP Six will want to ensure that their purchases are safe and secure. They will make purchases of highly respected and trustworthy institutions or brands that provide them with a sense that they are affiliated with powerful and worthy institutions. The CBP Six will be very interested in the safety features of a purchase and will want assurances that it will do what it says it will do.

## At home

### As a partner

The CBP Six can be very strong on ideas but they tend to be very weak on follow through. A romance that was initially interesting suddenly becomes doubtful. They can fall into a bind – if they go ahead they are going to be hurt but if they do not then they will miss out. This double-mindedness can appear to be ambivalence: they seem unable to make a commitment and when they do they continue to waver between doubt and belief. How can a relationship develop when there is no trust?

In a long-term relationship, the CBP Six must be able to air their concerns or else their worries will become fact within their mind.

Expressing doubt is a way to gain trust, even though this can cause real pain to a partner. But once trust is gained the CBP Six will become extremely loyal to their partner and will often shoulder a large degree of responsibility in the relationship (Palmer, 1995, pp164–166).

## Dos and don'ts

- The CBP Six can be a loyal supporter who adopts the position of us against the world.
- Do appreciate that a CBP Six will question your intentions, and be suspicious when you show you care, wondering what it is that you really think. This suspicion is not the most romantic mood.
- Do be aware that CBP Sixes will project their feelings of infidelity onto you, sensing that you are attracted to someone else.
- Do expect the CBP Six to identify with the problem areas of relationships which will then become the focus of their attention.
- Don't try to have an impact on the CBP Six. They want to have the impact on you (for example, through warmth, by sexual power or duty, or through giving the most to the relationship).
- Don't rely on the CBP Six to be aware of the source of tension in the relationship. They constantly expect to be hurt as soon as they drop their guard.
- Do reassure the CBP Six that underneath all the dialogue, they can trust you.

*(Adapted from Palmer, 1995, pp163–164)*

## As a child

As children, CBP Sixes report that they experienced the world as a dangerous or fearful place. Often it was the result of unpredictable parents or siblings. The danger could have taken an emotional, intellectual or physical form. The child observed that the powerful figures in their world could not be depended on for protection and security. As a result the child sought protection by scanning the environment for danger, through thinking before acting, by doubting self and others and through an augmented imagination (Palmer, 1988).

# CBP Six at their worst

The emotions of the CBP Six are manifested through the continuum of phobic to counter-phobic. The flight form of fear, through retreat or through compliance, is the phobic response while the confrontational and antiauthoritarian response is referred to as counter-phobic. While phobic CBP Sixes may be very present to their fear and seek to avoid it, the counterphobic CBP Six has absolutely no idea that they are fearful because they attack anything that they fear, flying in the face of the most dangerous situations. At their worst the CBP Six spends a lot of time in preparation for possible disasters. They are often thinking ahead to the worst-case scenario and anticipating it. The need for absolute certainty leads to endless planning and procrastination on the part of the CBP Six.

## Case study

Greene's story (1998, pp131–132), which exemplifies this profile is about the first Emperor of China, Ch'in Shih Huang Ti (221–210 BC), who was the most powerful man in the world. While his empire was greater and more mighty than that of any other, and his conquest and leadership gave rise to a unified China, he devolved into paranoia and despite his might, became a recluse.

Ch'in Shih Huang Ti had conquered the provinces surrounding his own and created China through trickery and violence. He dismantled the ancient feudal system and, to keep his eye on the various members of the old royal families, he displaced 120,000 of them to a place within his reach.

As part of his unification and motivated by his fear, he completed the wall building, creating the Great Wall of China. He was so suspicious of organised religion that he outlawed Confucianism, which was an authoritative philosophy in the land. He even destroyed the books of Confucius' writing and executed his followers. But this was not enough to assuage his fears caused by the hatred he had engendered in his subjects. A contemporary of the Emperor wrote that 'Ch'in has been victorious for four generations, yet has lived in constant terror and apprehension of destruction.'(Greene, 1998, p131).

He lived within the most beautiful palace that had ever been built, and he had all the power he wanted, and yet his paranoia knew no bounds.

Fearful of being seen by an assassin, he connected every room in the palace, sleeping in different rooms every night and beheading everyone who saw him.

Ch'in Shih Huang Ti had become so scared of human contact that when he needed to leave the palace he would travel in disguise. It was on one such occasion that he died, alone and far from his wives, his family, his friends, and his courtiers, accompanied only by a minister and a handful of eunuchs. His body was carried back to the capital with the cart packed with salted fish trailing behind it to cover up the smell of the rotting corpse. Even his death was to be hidden.

In giving in to his fear and retreating deeper into the palace to protect himself, Ch'in Shih Huang Ti had slowly lost control of the empire. In the end self-imposed isolation and fears meant that political decisions often had to be made by his ministers. So in the end he was Emperor in name only. Ch'in Shih Huang Ti's fear of conspiracies led him to a position where he was constantly surrounded by conspirators and was powerless to confront them.

## Exemplars of the type

| | |
|---|---|
| Bill Murray | Dick Smith |
| Meg Ryan | Jay Leno |
| John McEnroe | Tom Hanks |
| Mel Gibson | Robert Kennedy |
| Richard Nixon | Osama Bin Laden |
| Woody Allen | Russell Crowe |
| John Howard | Andrew Denton |
| John Pilger | Julia Roberts |
| Professor Alan Fels | Helen Hunt |

# Core Belief Profile Seven – Epicures

The Core Belief Profile Seven could be considered as a joyful person since they are highly optimistic, imaginative, ever hopeful and orientated towards pleasure. They focus on future plans and pleasant possibilities as a way of escaping the limitations of boredom and pain. The Core Belief Profile Seven has a fascination with others, with themselves and with the natural world. They will plan optimistically for the future along with a series of alternatives in case the initial plan becomes difficult or uninteresting.

The basic assumption of the Core Belief Profile Seven is that the painful control of others and of events can be escaped through a fast moving mind that moves on to more pleasant options. Their attention goes to many alternative pleasurable options, to interrelationships and to pursuing happiness. They are an assertive profile because they feel that anything meaningful happens in relation to them and that something is going to happen because of them. They demand the security that they are seeking. When a Core Belief Profile Seven walks into a room they subconsciously think, 'Here I am! Things are going to be more lively now!' The Core Belief Profile Seven is convinced of their own excellence and they seek environments and people who will support their worth.

## Emotional state

The Core Belief Profile Seven is formed around the emotion of gluttony for all the enjoyable experiences that life has to offer. Since they are focused on enjoying and experiencing life to its fullest, they try to move quickly from one thing to another. They will sample but not depth any experience, particularly if the experience could hold any emotional pain. A sense of absolute freedom without responsibility or commitment is the objective of this gluttony.

Since the Core Belief Profile Seven moves through life without depthing any experiences, particularly those that may cause pain, they never learn from their mistakes. Ultimately, they create painful situations for themselves because they never develop the insight to break the patterns that would allow them to experience things more deeply.

# Principal Characteristics – Profile Seven

## Focus of attention

- Interesting, pleasurable and fascinating ideas, plans, options, projects
- Interconnections and interrelationships among diverse areas of information and knowledge
- What they want

(Adapted from Daniels, et. al. 2000, p46)

## Focus of energy

- Enjoying and experiencing life to its fullest
- Keeping options open and life upbeat
- An active imagination
- Being liked (charming and disarming)
- Maintaining a privileged position

(Quoted from Daniels, et. al. 2000, p46)

## Focus of avoidance

- Frustrations, constraints and limitations
- Painful situations or feelings
- Boredom

(Quoted from Daniels, et. al. 2000, p46)

## Self-justifying reframes

- Playfulness
- Inventiveness
- Being enjoyable and upbeat
- High energy
- Optimism
- Love of life
- Vision
- Enthusiasm
- Helpfulness
- Imagination

## Weaknesses

- Gluttony
- Anticipating

## Preferred communication style

- Want to be intellectually inspired and excited; low tolerance for boredom or slow pace
- Attention goes to multiple options or shifts from one plan to the next very quickly
- Capable of synthesising large amounts of data and including divergent points of view
- Like a combination of learning modes; fast-paced thinking, processing and experiencing
- Prefer a quick overview and then to jump right into new material; not dependent on approval or establishing safety
- Most comfortable with a synergistic and divergent approach

## Key words and traits

- Gluttony
- Hedonistic permissiveness
- Rebelliousness
- Lack of discipline
- Imaginary wish fulfilment
- Seductively pleasing
- Narcissism
- Fraudulence

## Other Names for this Type

- Adventurers
- New Adopters
- Pleasure-Seeker

## At work

- The dos and don'ts of working with Sevens
- Do prepare for rapid give and take on issues. The CBP Seven will talk fast and think fast. Keep in mind that this is just possibly talk, not actual commitment. If you want commitment then ensure that you get it in writing. A handshake and a smile is not sufficient.
- Do align with their dream. Let the CBP Seven share their vision and enthusiasm with you. They will feel supported when another acknowledges their individuality, experimentation and creativity.
- Don't focus on small and picky details.
- Do ask lots of questions. The CBP Seven loves hypothesising and answering questions.
- Do share your problem with the CBP Seven rather than internalising it or judging them. CBP Sevens like being part of the process; what you see as a problem they may see as an interesting opportunity.

*(Adapted from Goldberg, 1999, p229)*

## Managing yourself as a Seven

- Be sure to constantly ask yourself, 'What are the plausible negatives on this project?' Then find ways of dealing with them.
- Under-promise. Sevens tend to over-promise because it gives them pleasure and they do not want to disappoint in the moment.
- Take small practical steps to bring your dreams into fruition – and then act on them.
- Learn to endure the consequences of your choices rather than simply changing paths midstream.
- Just because an idea has come into your head, it does not have to be expressed.
- Curb your tendency to make fun of people, to treat them carelessly, and to tell them to get over their problems and lighten up.
- Think about closure in advance.
- Be aware of your tendency to rationalise, to explain away failure and ethical violations without taking responsibility.

- Develop the skill of really listening rather than trying to think of something clever to say later.
- Work! Actually get your work completed rather than thinking about what else you could be doing.
- Practise mental sobriety. Do not just become drunk on ideas.

## As a customer

The CBP Seven tends to make impulse purchases of new or fascinating products. The CBP Seven is constantly looking for new experiences – any product or service that provides a new experience will be appreciated. The CBP Seven is particularly attracted to the shiny new product or service. That is, they value the brand new, and in this regard it is important that the packaging appeal to the notion that this is quirky and different.

## At home

### As a partner

The CBP Seven appears to be upbeat in relationships. Since they have difficulties staying with negative emotions, it is almost impossible for them to remain present and to feel bad. Their mind almost immediately moves on to positive options. They will try to find many different solutions and many exits before they reach the point of anger. In a relationship, it is difficult to pin them into a corner when they are trying to find a way out.

Surface relationships can be a lot more fun than those that demand emotional engagement. But it is important for CBP Sevens to have relationships that are dedicated to real work (Palmer, 1995, pp188–190).

*(Adapted from Goldberg, 1999, pp229–230)*

### Dos and don'ts

- Do mirror the CBP Seven's own high self-image.
- Do admire them. This makes the CBP Seven very pleasant company.
- Do expect that they will ridicule or discount you or the situation when they are challenged or made to feel inferior.

- Do anticipate anger if you attempt to control the movement of the CBP Seven. They want to move with the flow and not be contained to any particular activity or event.
- The CBP Seven likes variety in all things, including intimacy. They will be interested in your personality and aspirations with depth, and will want to enjoy many different activities with you.

## As a child

As children, CBP Sevens typically report being happy and having an enjoyable childhood. These memories take on a storybook quality with very little suffering or bitterness. They were affirmed by their parents for being positive, enjoyable and optimistic, and discouraged for expressing pain or suffering. Sometimes a childhood is remembered as painful but the child's role was to be happy and optimistic. As a result the child developed a strong sense of self-worth and importance while focusing on pleasant options, optimistic outcomes, planning the future and avoiding pain and suffering (Palmer, 1988).

## CBP Seven at their worst

In the presence of being trapped or controlled the emotions of the CBP Seven will force them to move quickly from one thing to another, sampling but never deepening any particular experience. This is particularly true if the experience could result in emotional pain. CBP Seven manifests as gluttony for new, fun and enjoyable experiences. Life is like a smorgasbord and is experienced as a range of experiences rather than a single experience repeated often. At their worst, they will seek absolute freedom without responsibility or commitment.

*(Adapted from Palmer, 1995, pp187–188)*

## Case study

This story from Greene (1998, pp368–369) shows the pathology of this Core Belief Profile. Marie-Antoinette married the heir-apparent to the French throne towards the end of the reign of Louis XV. The people welcomed her in anticipation of her reign. 'How fortunate,' she wrote her mother, 'to be in a position in which one can gain widespread affection at so little cost.' But she grew to take this affection for granted (Greene, 1998, p368).

It was in 1774 that Louis XVI ascended the throne but the new Queen gave in to unending pleasures, extravagant gowns and jewellery, parties and fetes, without concerning herself who would foot the bill. Her search for pleasures and self-indulgence went so far that she created her own make-believe garden, where poverty and pain were absent. So she had no interest in the plight of the French people, struggling under poverty and hardship. Of course, she neglected her duties to her subjects. In her egocentricity and conceit she believed it was not her necessity to earn their respect and affection.

Once it became public knowledge about how much money Marie-Antoinette spent on jewels and dresses and masked dances, she was given the name 'Madame Deficit.' She became the focal point of the public's rapidly rising resentment.

It was in 1789 that the French Revolution started. The Queen was completely without fear. She is reported to have said, 'Let the people have their little rebellion. It will soon quiet down.' She believed that this was a minor interruption to her pleasurable life. But, of course, it wasn't. Both King and Queen were executed. Her pleasurable life came to an end without any sympathy from anyone. The unrepentant Queen went to the guillotine unchanged.

## Exemplars of the type

| | |
|---|---|
| Bill Clinton | Billy Connolly |
| Barry Jones | David Suzuki |
| Goldie Hawn | Paul McDermott |
| Timothy Leary | Richard Branson |
| Joan Rivers | Cameron Diaz |
| Jack Nicholson | Sarah Ferguson |
| David Attenborough | Kate Winslet |
| Robin Williams | |

# Core Belief Profile Eight – The Boss

The Core Belief Profile Eight could be considered the powerful person as they are personally assertive and seek to control their immediate environment. The Core Belief Profile Eight focuses on being strong and powerful in response to an unjust world. They do this through control and dominance of their personal space and of the people within their space. They use confrontations with others to establish the truth, and they focus on the weaknesses of others and their own strengths to establish their control over their environment.

The basic assumption is that any weakness will be used to control them – just as they try to use the weaknesses of others to control them. The reason that they are assertive is because they seek to protect themselves and others to gain respect while also hiding any weakness or vulnerability that may lead to betrayal and injustice. The focus of attention is outward and based around perceived power. Core Belief Profile Eight is an assertive profile in that it demands the autonomy that it seeks. They are very passionate about whatever actions or activity they are engaged with.

## Emotional state

The Core Belief Profile Eight is formed around the emotion of lust, as it is a desire for intensity in all things. Moderation is death, and if something is good, then they cannot have enough. With relationships, they will be possessive towards friends and intimates and will often try to take over. The lust for friendship has to do with camaraderie as they want to know that what is said is said in the spirit of friendship and they will be taken care of. Lust is a craving for satisfaction and when something desirable comes to mind, they are not particularly aware of the consequences of what they say or do. Once the goal is set, obstacles seem minimal and their task is to get what they want in the most expedient way possible. Intensity is created when the Core Belief Profile Eight believes that they are being taken advantage of. It also creates a sense of speed, cleverness and strength of will.

Since the Core Belief Profile Eight has a world view in which the strong survive and the weak do not, they have a deep suspicion of ambiguity or mixed messages because they see them as weak. Their desire to maintain control plays a part in their preoccupation with justice.

# Principal Characteristics – Profile Eight

## Focus of attention

- Power and control
- Justice and injustice
- Deceptions and manipulations
- All-or-nothing polarities
- Whatever demands action right now

    (Quoted from Daniels, et. al. 2000, p50)

## Focus of energy

- Control and dominance of their space and of the people and things in their space
- Taking direct action and facing conflict
- Protecting the weak and innocent
- Gaining respect by being strong and just

    (Adapted from Daniels et al, 2000, p50)

## Focus of avoidance

- Being weak, vulnerable, uncertain or dependent
- Losing the regard of people they respect

    (Adapted from Daniels, et. al. 2000, p50)

## Self-justifying reframes

- Courage
- Persistence
- Fairness
- Decisiveness
- Protectiveness
- Self-assertion
- Intensity
- Friendliness
- The ability to energise others

## Weaknesses

- Too worked up
- Overcharged

## Preferred communication style

- Want to see the big picture and how the parts relate to the whole
- Want a balance of theory and application
- Want clarity, focus and a defined structure in establishing the learning environment
- Want to move quickly to the substance of the material after a brief initial opening
- Want energetic and lively learning situations; no tolerance for boredom
- The enjoyment of the communication interaction may be as important as the actual content
- Expects the instructor/manager to engage in dialogue and to tolerate some amount of conflict, even while holding their position
- Doesn't want to feel confined; likes to be able to get up and move around the room
- Prefers multi-dimensional learning, and/or body-based learning

## Key words and traits

- Lust
- Punitive
- Rebellious
- Dominance
- Insensitive
- Exhibitionist
- Autonomy
- Sensor motor dominance

## Other Names for this Type

- Protectors

The Core Belief Profile Eight applies pressure to discover people's real motivations, and their self-concept is as a defender of the weak.

## At work

- The dos and don'ts of working with Eights
- Do ensure that you always turn up when you are expected to.
- Do articulate yourself confidently. CBP Eights appreciate news straight up and to the point. Do not waffle. Do not embellish.
- Don't complain about the results. They do not want to hear your excuses – they want results.
- Do give the CBP Eight your respect. They want respect for being a substantial figure, not a petty functionary.
- Do understand that if an Eight gives you a verbal tongue lashing, do not simply blast back. Standing up to them is different from raising the stakes, which gives the Eight no option but to try and annihilate them. Instead, acknowledge their power but also remind them of your own.
- Do provide explanations for problems in black and white terms. CBP Eights have little tolerance for subtlety or philosophical context.
- Do you need this fight? If not, close the deal without that element.
- Ask yourself, 'Is this clause essential to the deal?' If it is, then explain to the Eight that it is a deal breaker and be prepared to back it up.
- Instead of holding on to your anger and resentment, do realise that they will always prefer that you tell them straight away when they are making mistakes or making you mad.

*(Adapted from Goldberg, 1999, pp260–261)*

## Managing yourself as an Eight

- Feeling as if someone is taking advantage of you is not the same as someone actually taking advantage of you. Check the details before you automatically retaliate.
- Choose your battles. Ask yourself, 'Is this fight worth it?'
- Before you totally attack someone, ask yourself whether you are willing to deal with the consequences.

- For many people, your threats and tirades are not effective, no matter how much you may enjoy putting them on.
- When giving instructions, be very specific about the behaviour that will satisfy your expectations.
- Find ways to use others' talents and give them a sense of ownership and empowerment rather than just being a hired hand.

*(Adapted from Goldberg, 1999, pp261–262)*

## As a customer

The CBP Eight will purchase goods and services based on the motto bigger is better. They want the biggest ute, the loudest stereo system, the most of whatever they are purchasing. Quality, reliability or any form of restraint are not issues that will make the CBP Eight make a purchase. If they like something, then they will want a double serving of it.

## At home

### As a partner

A main concern of the CBP Eight is personal freedom, and they are often convinced that dependency can make them powerless. They will often confuse tenderness for dependency and so they can be inexperienced with the softer feelings of romance. The CBP Eight tends to reinvigorate their relationships with conflict, activity, adventure or sex; yet they can be very sensitive to rejection in a relationship.

Relating to a CBP Eight requires confrontation. They feel they must test your limits. They have to know that it is safe to surrender control. Anger can erupt about trivial issues, since the central issue is actually power and the conflict is just a means to test who has it (Palmer, 1995, pp212–213).

*(Adapted from Goldberg, 1999, pp261–262)*

## Dos and don'ts

- Do expect everything to happen to excess. They have an all or nothing approach. It is either all work, where only work will be considered, or all play and absolutely nothing will get done.
- Do be independent and strong as CBP Eights like these qualities in a partner.
- The CBP Eight enjoys fighting, sex and adventure as ways of making contact.
- Do understand that the CBP Eight expresses their power through episodes of strict control followed by disobedience. They like to make the rules and then they break them to keep life interesting.
- Don't try to control them. Their fear of being controlled becomes transferred onto the territorial control of objects or physical space.
- Don't let yourself have small oversights. Because CBP Eights cannot tolerate ambiguity, small oversights can seem to be betrayals of trust.
- Do appreciate that if the CBP Eight feels that they have been betrayed then they will go out of their way to achieve a sense of revenge. This is particularly true if they have felt that they made themselves vulnerable in a relationship only to be betrayed.
- Do appreciate that the CBP Eight is a tower of strength in times of trouble, a formidable friend.

*(Adapted from Palmer, 1995, pp211–212)*

## As a child

CBP Eights often report a combative childhood. In most cases the source of threat may have been physical and the CBP Eight learned that strength was respected while weakness was not. Often they perceived one parent as being strong and the other as being weak. The child was sometimes against the odds and the young CBP Eight learned to be self-reliant and to fight for justice. As a result they grew to depend on no one but themselves, to be strong or assertive and avoid vulnerability or weakness (Palmer, 1988).

*(Adapted from Palmer, 1995, pp211–212)*

## CBP Eight at their worst

At their worst the CBP Eight will entertain an enormous lust for life. They will seek intensity in all things as the hallmark of a fulfilling life. If they enjoy something, then there can never be enough. They always want more. Moderation is death when the emotion of the CBP Eight is high. Always they want more, better, faster and louder. This sometimes leads to difficulty with people or friends who cannot 'keep up' with their energy.

This intensity is used to control others through the creation of physical, material or emotional dependence. Intensity sorts out the strong from the weak. This CBP reports that most people fall into two categories – those that can't help being weak and those that can.

### Case study

This Core Belief is exemplified in the life of Ivan the Terrible. Born in 1530, Ivan was only three when he inherited the Russian throne following his father's death. By the age of eight, he was an orphan. He was isolated and with only one friend, and physically and emotionally abused by the Shuisky family, rivals to the throne.

It was around this time that his cruelty to both animals and people became evident. Not only was he a cruel man, it also gave him pleasure to see the pain of others. All this behaviour was driven by his anger, but made excessive in expression by his passion and lust for life.

After his wife's death, Ivan's sense of cruelty and revenge against his perceived enemies was magnified. His moods oscillated between anger and hatred to piety and remorse. So there were endless stories of cruelty along with religious rituals that included sexual orgies, dismembering and mock piety.

In his state of mad rage, Ivan would not hesitate to burn a whole city and kill its citizens in the most bestial ways, as reported by eye-witness accounts of survivors.

Eventually Ivan killed his own son for defending his pregnant wife against her father's wrath.

Poisoned by mercury, Ivan died in a state of remorse, dressed in a monk's habit and re-christened, hoping for forgiveness of his sins.

## Exemplars of the type

- Kerry Packer
- Steve Irwin
- Mikhail Gorbachev
- Martin Luther King
- Barbara Walters
- Bette Davis
- Indira Gandhi
- John Wayne
- Dawn Fraser

- Golda Meir
- Yitzak Rabin
- Fidel Castro
- John Elliott
- Fred Hollows
- Wilson Tuckey
- Ariel Sharon
- Barbara Walters
- Courtney Love

# Core Belief Profile Nine – Peacemakers

The Core Belief Profile Nine is the peaceful person as they have the stylised image that they are settled and relaxed. They are even-tempered, harmonious, relaxed, unflappable and unpretentious. The Core Belief Profile Nine focuses on being sensitive to others and their agendas as well as on keeping life comfortable and familiar. This leads to an avoidance of overt conflict and a tendency to accept the wishes of others by forgetting their own needs. Change is always postponed in order to avoid anger and separation.

The underlying assumption is that the world treats people as unimportant for what they are, and they are required to blend in as the way to experience a sense of comfort and belonging. As a consequence they will avoid conflict, which is not only avoiding becoming angry but also an avoidance of anything uncomfortable. This can manifest itself through a need to make the peace in every situation, and this will tend to be expressed as a soothing and peaceful environment. The Core Belief Profile Nine is a withdrawing profile as they will go into a safe and carefree inner sanctum in their minds rather than getting out of their imaginations and into action.

## Emotional state

The Core Belief Profile Nine is formed around the emotion of slothfulness. This gives rise to much listening and absorbing but no discernment. This is referred to as slothfulness as it means being intellectually lazy. Decisions are difficult as Nines can see all sides of an issue. In particular, the slothfulness revolves around indecisiveness about personal priorities, particularly if it has any basis in building self-esteem or self-worth.

The Core Belief Profile Nine experiences anger and resentment over the feeling that they are being ignored. Since they try to avoid conflict, and any strong emotion is considered to give rise to conflict, the Core Belief Profile Nines try to suppress all personal emotions. They also have a strong fear of anger, their own or another person's, and of uncomfortable situations.

# Principal Characteristics – Profile Nine

## Focus of attention
- Others' agendas, requests and demands
- All the things in the environment that beckon

  (Quoted from Daniels, et. al. 2000, p54)

## Focus of energy
- Being sensitive to others and trying to please them
- Keeping life comfortable and familiar
- Maintaining structure and routine so that life will be predictable
- Maintaining peace and quiet
- Containing anger
- Doing the less essential and comforting activities rather than the more important and more disturbing ones

  (Quoted from Daniels, et. al. 2000, p54)

## Focus of avoidance
- Conflict, confrontation, feeling uncomfortable
- Too many competing demands on their attention and energy

  (Adapted from Daniels, et. al. 2000, p54)

## Self-justifying reframes
- Attentiveness to others
- Empathy
- Supportiveness
- Accountability
- Steadfastness
- Adaptive
- Accepting
- Receptive
- Caring

## Weaknesses
- Sloth
- Non-self-consciousness

## Preferred communication style
- Likes to see the big picture and how all the parts relate to the whole, and looks for the underlying patterns of unity and cohesion
- Can also take time to thoroughly examine each detail and complete the necessary work in sequence
- May have trouble shifting attention back and forth from specifics to the big picture, or differentiating foreground and background
- May have difficulty focusing attention on the priority
- Sense of camaraderie with others is important; needs to respect the instructor/manager, but a personal relationship is not necessary
- Needs to feel comfortable in the environment in order to relax into the learning
- Access point to learning is through the physical sense of activity, other people and the environment

## Key words and traits
- Psychological/spiritual inertia
- Over-adaptation
- Resignation
- Generosity
- Ordinariness
- Distractibility

# At work

## The dos and don'ts of working with Nines

- Do understand that the CBP Nine never makes fixed commitments as they are always filled with contingency. Confirm the decisions and then the follow-up details that you want them to follow.
- Don't mistake their silence for agreement.
- Don't take a yes for an answer either; they may not even know they do not mean it. Find out what they really think is possible.
- Do appreciate that CBP Nines hate pomposity and pretension. They are naturally humble and want you to be as well.
- Do establish very clear performance goals. They tend to get fuzzy and forgetful when it comes to agreements, so it is good to have them in writing. It is best if the CBP Nine does the writing.
- Do listen for the CBP Nine to convince themselves that they are not important, as this is one reason that they do not follow up very well.
- They need to be reminded that their assignments are important, that they themselves are important, and that other people will be disadvantaged if they do not do their job well.
- Realise that asking a Nine for their opinion is one way to get them on board.
- Do provide CBP Nines with regular meetings. CBP Nines will not assert themselves to claim the time they need, but they do very well when they have your undivided attention. CBP Nines will feel that they are not important if you are distracted by phone calls or other interruptions.

*(Adapted from Goldberg, 1999, pp293–294)*

# Managing yourself as a Nine

- Don't ask what you need to do next, rather ask what you need to finish next. Then go about finishing it.
- Write a mission statement for each of your projects to clarify where you are going and why. Do the same for your life.
- Learn to tolerate the discomfort of desire. Follow your passions

and set personal goals for yourself.

- Don't leave less desirable options in play. Play them or eliminate them.
- Do not let decisions that can be made drag on.
- Ask yourself in each issue, 'Is it actually my issue, or have I unnecessarily taken on someone else's problem as my own?'
- Narrow your focus.
- State what you have to say without qualifying it or undermining it.
- When you hear yourself equivocating, stop. Learn to be specific and direct. And do not feel obliged to repeat yourself.
- Don't ignore your employee's requests for a decision. Sometimes they do in fact require real guidance.
- Don't give everything away. Own some of the credit, the authority, or the influence.

*(Adapted from Goldberg, 1999, pp294–295)*

## As a customer

The CBP Nine will focus on purchases that are comfortable. They will look for goods and services that ease the pain of life by making the journey smoother. For the CBP Nine it will be comfort that provides the overriding reason for the purchasing decision.

## At home

### As a partner

The CBP Nine seems to know other people's wishes much more clearly than they know their own. It is easier for them to step into someone else's shoes and to see through their eyes but difficult to decide for themselves. Having your own position means having to defend it, and this is so very rarely worth the effort or the risk of alienating those you love. The indecisiveness of a CBP Nine can be a challenge for partners who are seeking leadership, since the Nine can so clearly see the arguments of both sides and so can come to no categorical conclusion.

While the CBP Nine may not know what they want they do know what they don't want. They don't want anything that will make them uncomfortable and so while they do not proffer positive options they will make their own desires felt by rejecting other options. If they feel they are being forced into a decision, the CBP Nine will become stubborn. They control through non-action (Palmer, 1995, pp236–238).

## Dos and don'ts

- Do realise that once a CBP Nine merges with you it is hard to separate.
- They tend to cling to a relationship long past its use-by date.
- Do realise that CBP Nines will side-track themselves from feelings by becoming preoccupied with non-essentials. They will discuss options to avoid conflict and may appear uninterested or withdrawn.
- Do appreciate that CBP Nines retreat into habitual patterns and mundane concerns rather than facing the hard work of engaging in the relationship. It will be up to you to initiate change.
- Don't believe that what the CBP Nine says is their opinion. They will frequently say back to you what it is that you want to hear, and your needs seem louder than theirs.
- Do be aware that for a deeper relationship, if the CBP Nine merges with you they need to also keep their own identity.

*(Adapted from Palmer, 1995, pp235–236)*

## As a child

As children, CBP Nines report that they felt overlooked or unheard. Usually they report that another sibling or a parent (or both) dominated the environment so completely that there was little room left for the CBP Nine. As a result the child learnt to know others' agendas better than their own. They learnt to forget themselves and to identify with others. The resentment and energy that arises at never being heard or acknowledged is diffused by the child into secondary or inessential pursuits and into a comfortable and predictable life (Palmer, 1988).

## CBP Nine at their worst

For the CBP Nine, at their worst they become very lazy about the important things that they have decided for themselves. This is particularly true if the thing that they have decided has any basis in building self-esteem or a sense of self-worth.

Their slothfulness takes the form of indecisiveness about personal priorities and positions. They avoid anger by minimising personal desire in favour of conflict minimisation. This behaviour often occurs as a feeling of being overwhelmed by life's details and distractions to the point where work on oneself is almost impossible. Finally, inertia plays a big part in keeping the CBP Nine at their worst. This allows them to routinely continue doing whatever they are comfortable with to the exclusion of the tasks that may be emotionally unsettling.

## Case study

Greene (1998, pp9–11) tells the story of Michael III. Around 950AD, Michael III became the Emperor of the Byzantine Empire. His ascension occurred after his mother, the Empress Theodora, had been banished to a nunnery and her lover, Theoctistus, had been murdered. The conspiracy that placed Michael III on the throne had been orchestrated by his uncle Bardas. At a time when he was himself an inexperienced ruler and surrounded by intriguers, murderers and profligates, Michael needed someone experienced he could trust. Rather than face the difficult experience of becoming a ruler, he chose his best friend Basilius.

Basilius had absolutely no experience in government or in politics. His experience had been as the head of the royal stables, but he had proven his love and gratitude to Michael time and time again.

The two had met a few years before, when Michael had been visiting the stables just as a wild horse escaped control. A young groom from peasant Macedonian stock saved Michael's life. That groom was Basilius. It was his strength and courage that impressed Michael the most and that encouraged him to raise Basilius from obscurity to the position of head of the stables. Michael provided Basilius with countless gifts and favours and the two became inseparable companions. As a result of this patronage, Basilius received a formal education and was transformed into a polished courtier.

Once he was elevated to the position of Emperor, Michael ignored advice urging him to put his qualified uncle Bardas in the important position of chamberlain and chief councillor and instead installed Basilius. The Macedonian learned quickly and he was soon advising the Emperor on all matters of state. The only source of difficulty in the relationship seemed to be over money – Basilius never seemed to have enough. When he saw the riches of the Byzantine court, he became avaricious and demanded more and more money and perks. Michael repeatedly failed to be assertive in the face of these demands and pacified his trusted friend by granting his every wish.

Basilius even went so far as to convince Michael that his uncle Bardas, who was now head of the army, was a potential conspirator. He forced Michael to agree to having his uncle killed and finally, during a horse race, Basilius stabbed Bardas to death. Basilius then became the head of the army and controlled the government.

When Michael later got into financial difficulties, he asked Basilius to repay what he owed him. However, Basilius refused and, knowing that the Emperor had no real power or strength of character, he had him killed in his sleep.

Michael's inability to objectively assess the conflict implicit in the struggle of power with his friend, and to confront it, led him to his own death.

Michael's life demonstrates that maintaining peace at any price is counterproductive and even catastrophic. Michael's passivity deprived the empire of a true successive monarch. Instead, it passed to another usurper and emotional manipulator.

## Exemplars of the type

- Alexander Downer
- Ronald Reagan
- Kevin Costner
- Kim Beazley
- Whoopi Goldberg
- Ricky May
- Matt Damon
- George Lucas
- Carl Jung
- Phil Koperberg
- Sophia Loren
- Geena Davis
- Lisa Kudrow
- Janet Jackson
- Nancy Kerrigan

# CHAPTER THREE
# Applying Core Beliefs to Business Challenges

Core Belief Research is increasingly being adopted by significant public companies and corporations to deliver fast and accurate insight into the way their stakeholders will react to a communications campaign or strategy. It provides valuable intelligence that can be applied in the following areas:

- Strategy Development or Strategic Alignment;
- Issues and Crises Planning and Management;
- Shareholder Communications;
- Board, CEO and Executive Team Alignment;
- Media Audits;
- Product Launches;
- Marketing and Communications;
- Community Consultation; and
- Internal Communications.

## Situations where Core Belief research shines

Organisations needing to address a specific challenge with one or more of their stakeholders, find Core Belief research particularly powerful when dealing with 'hot' issues such as:

- Addressing shareholders at an AGM on a difficult issue;
- Dealing with a crisis concerning a product in the market;
- Exploring why certain customers are reluctant to buy a service or product;
- Communicating with employees during a downsizing;
- Gaining support for a controversial community-based action;
- Launching a new product or service;
- Influencing key media in their industry sector; and
- Increasing the hit-rate on new business development.

# Case studies

## Community benchmarking for the timber industry

An Australian State Government wanted to change community attitudes about the timber industry and the perception of the impact of logging on the environment. We researched the Core Beliefs of the community regarding the timber industry and developed a communications strategy that was Core Belief aligned. Twelve months later, our post-strategy research revealed that community support of the State Government's vision for forests had moved from just 25 per cent to 90 per cent.

## Dealing with reluctant customers

A client in the personal insurance sector wanted to understand their 'reluctant customer base' and develop marketing communications that would encourage them to stay loyal even if their premium prices were increased. We analysed the Core Belief Profiles of the customer base and developed marketing recommendations that addressed their communication and motivational needs. This enabled them to not only increase their premium by 30 per cent but also increase their customer base by five per cent.

## Managing shareholder outcome for a multinational financial leader

A large insurance company, which had been the subject of a hostile takeover, had to inform their shareholders of complex material and then guide them to vote appropriately in a highly volatile environment and under the pressure of media scrutiny. Core Belief research identified how the various types of shareholders preferred to receive information, how they interpreted this information and how they responded to it. It also identified key elements of shareholder sentiment and took into account the daily media reporting and how it was affecting public opinion. A strategy was developed to manage the process, develop key messages, write documentation, speeches and media content which all linked into the positive Core Beliefs of the shareholders.

The outcome was outstanding. Over a period of seven weeks shareholder support of the Scheme of Arrangement increased from 22 per cent to 98 per cent. The shareholder meeting was conducted in a calm and non-confrontational environment, media coverage was balanced and the company executive team gained credibility and respect.

**Organisations that have used the Core Belief framework to drive engagement and performance in their business:**

## Australian

AMP | ARUP | Australian Institute of Customer Service | Arts Queensland | BHP Billiton | BMA Coal | Boyne Smelters | Brainmates | City of South Perth | City of Mandurah | Corporate Air Services | Commonwealth Bank | Credit Union Australia | Dairy Farmers Co-Op | Department of Primary Industries | EDS Australia | Electaserv | Environmental Protection Agency | Forest Products Commission WA | Franklin Covey Middle East | George Patterson Y&R | GE Money | Great Barrier Reef Marine Park Authority | HSBC | Local Government Association WA | Main Roads Qld | Macquarie Bank | NRMA | NSW Rail Infrastructure Corporation | Pacific Coal | Performance Frontiers | PricewaterhouseCoopers | QMI Solutions | Queensland Health | Queensland Motorways | Queensland Museum | Queensland Rail | QRNational | Queensland Sugar | Queensland Transport | Queensland Womens Legal Service | Rigby Cooke Lawyers | Rio Tinto Alcan | RACWA | Royal Melbourne Institute of Technology | Stryker | Suncorp Group of Companies | The Difference | Thiess | Trilby Misso Lawyers | Unisys | Vale Australia | Virgin Blue | Vision Personal Training | Westpac | Whitbread Insurance

Apple Computer | Boeing | Cisco Systems | Disney | General Motors | Hewlett Packard | Hyatt Hotels | Kare Coaching India | KLM | Kodak | Lucent

## International

Technologies | Marriott Hotels | Mondo Consulting Malaysia | Motorola | PeopleSoft | Phillips Electronics | Proctor & Gamble | Prudential | Reebok | Shell | Sony | Sun Microsystems | Xerox

# CHAPTER FOUR
# The Power of Core Beliefs
# in Your Organisation

NeuroPower is a consulting firm offering Core Belief research as the basis of stakeholder analysis for innovative leaders and corporate decision-makers who wish to understand, in more depth and with greater accuracy, how their stakeholders, including leadership teams, employees, clients, shareholders, financiers, customers and community will respond to strategic actions and information.

Core Belief research provides fast, accurate insight into stakeholder behaviour giving companies the latest business intelligence based on the latest findings in neuroscience to achieve their corporate goals. This insight can be used throughout an organisation from the Board and leadership team to investor relations, HR, public affairs, corporate communications, marketing and sales.

The power of Core Beliefs research lies in its ability to cut across the various segmentation models on offer, revealing that behaviour has a surer link to Core Beliefs than it has to commonly used parameters such as age, income, education, culture and socio-economic status.

## The key to Core Beliefs is predictability

If you can predict the behaviour – as opposed to the attitude – of a group, you can confidently plan for the best and prepare for the worst. Core Beliefs offer unprecedented insight into the underlying drivers, behavioural patterns and habitual responses of individuals, groups and cultures.

Using the Core Belief framework as the underlying structure we can not only predict behaviour, but also ensure the key stakeholder groups align with your strategic direction. We do this by using Core Beliefs to drive a range of specific solutions.

These solutions include:

## 1. Communications

Our experience has demonstrated that communication is usually the primary challenge facing both corporations and government bodies alike. Despite best efforts, communication often becomes a 'hit and miss affair' with communications departments unable to influence senior management of its importance and unable to get the desired cut through that is needed to be effective.

**Internal** – The Core Belief framework enables NeuroPower to develop tailored internal communication strategies that are based on the specific Core Belief Profile of an organisation. This means that corporate communication is tailored in the method of delivery, type of information, look and feel of the medium and frequency of contact. They are all designed to talk directly to the 'Organisational Profile'. Just as importantly, the keywords, phrases and themes that will negatively 'trigger' the Core Beliefs of the employees are flagged to ensure that they are not used informally by managers or in internal communications. This dual approach ensures leader believability and credibility and reduces employee resistance to both the message and change.

**Customers** – Understanding your customer's motivation to buy your goods or services is an area that has been approached from every angle since time immemorial. Applying the Core Belief framework enables us to give you an in-depth analysis of what would attract a customer to your offerings and why they will buy from you over another supplier. Core Beliefs also enable you to see which profiles your product or service will attract and which it won't, and how to direct your marketing and promotion to focus on those who are most likely to want to buy.

**Stakeholders** – Whether they are shareholders, members or partners, the way you communicate with them can have a major impact on the strategic direction and the bottom line of your business. Using the Core Belief framework, we can audit your existing communications, research the 'profile' of the target group and advise how you can tailor your communications to show that the organisational direction is in line with their internal drivers.

## 2. Organisational and cultural change, productivity and workforces

An understanding of the Core Beliefs of your employees will give your organisation a competitive advantage, remove the barriers to employee engagement and give access to the magic bullet that all organisations are looking for – 'discretionary effort'. In this day and age most organisations have wrung every bit of productivity out of their systems and processes. Discretionary effort is not something that can be demanded of an employee.

Instead, discretionary effort is the consequence of employees embracing the strategic direction of the organisation because they feel as if they 'belong' and are making a valuable contribution.

Using Core Beliefs, the leadership team is able to understand and remove the barriers preventing full employee engagement.

NeuroPower can also give clients access to a **cultural change** program, based on Core Beliefs, which makes a world of difference in engaging a workforce. If you can predict and track behaviour, you can create your desired culture by removing the Core Belief barriers. This can save millions in rolling out the wrong 'off the shelf' cultural change program.

## 3. Hiring

Hiring the right people for the right job is vital to the success and future of any organisation. This can be hit and miss sometimes as often what people say in an interview is only what *they believe you want to hear*. You hire them on *what they say* and can then be disappointed by *what they do*. Using Core Beliefs in the interview process can take a lot of the guesswork and angst out of the recruitment process. By providing an understanding of the prospects' inherent behavioural patterns, we are able to advise their fit to the job, the areas in which they will excel and the areas that will challenge them. This means that when you hire the person, you are entering into the relationship with your eyes wide open and are able to create an environment that will bring out the best in the employee and address the areas that they may find difficult.

## 4. Staff retention

Keeping good staff these days seems like an impossible task. The average length of a career is five years with some executive positions turning over every eighteen months. Usually good people don't leave an organisation, they leave people. Our research shows that a manager's lack of understanding of the differences in the operational drivers (Core Beliefs) of employees is a key factor in staff turnover. This major issue can be easily rectified by appropriate training.

## 5. Personal and professional development

Providing ongoing personal and professional development for employees is a key part of employee retention and Human Resource Management best practice. Using Core Beliefs training as part of a development program gives employees insight into the repeating patterns (habitual responses) of their leadership style and their blind spots. NeuroPower offers individual and group training in Core Beliefs and the best way to apply this to Executive Presentation Skills, Conflict Resolution, Negotiation, Team Building and Leadership Skills.

## 6. Safety

By applying the Core Belief framework we are able to create a cultural map that will give powerful understanding of the behavioural drivers of the workforce. Using this cultural map as a point of reference, we can then audit safety and induction programs, training programs, signage and all other safety related material to determine how aligned it is with the workforce's world view and make specific, practical recommendations to realign it.

## 7. Media presentation and reputation management

The public perception of your organisation is largely in the hands of the media. This is a big statement, but not far off the money. If you perform well as an organisation but poorly in the media, you will be perceived by the public at large as a poor performer whether you like it or not. (This is because the media is usually the only access the public has to your organisation and is seen as a credible, independent source of information.) This will have a negative impact on the organisation's reputation, which impacts on client and customer confidence, and in the case of listed companies, has a negative impact on share price.

Unfortunately, many organisations try to stay out of and ignore the media, preferring to 'keep their heads down' in case they get hit by a 'stray bullet'. This means that the great work they do is never heard about, and they miss out on many opportunities to showcase the very reasons they are in business.

Using an understanding of Core Beliefs, we demystify the media and show how to use it to the advantage of the organisation. If you understand *what* the public is looking for, *why* they believe what they do about you, and *how* they perceive you, you are able to create a public image that appeals to and aligns with the Core Beliefs of the general population. NeuroPower runs one to five day training programs in all areas of media, and partners with clients on an ongoing basis to keep them aligned with the world view of 'Stakeholder Joe'.

These are just some of the commercial applications of the Core Belief framework.

If you would like more information on using Core Beliefs in your organisation to gain insight, build reputation and increase performance, contact us at NeuroPower as per our details on page 88.

# Bibliography

Belch, G.E., and Belch, M.A., *Advertising and Promotion: An Integrated Marketing Communications Perspective*. Irwin/Mcgraw-Hill Series in Marketing, 1999.

Burow, P.L., and Burke, D.J., *Creating Performance Cultures within Organisations,* Australian Institute for Enneagram Studies, Unpublished.

Cahill, L., et al., *Beta-adrenergic Activation and Memory for Emotional Events,* Nature, October, 1994.

Chalmers, D.J., *The Conscious Mind,* New York: Oxford University Press, 1996.

Cohen, J., *A Power Primer,* Psychological Bulletin, 112, 155, 159, 1992.

Cohen, J., *Statistical Power Analysis for the Behavioural Sciences,* New York: Academic Press, 1969.

Daniels, D. and Price, V., *The Essential Enneagram: The Definitive Personality Test and Self-Discovery Guide,* HarperCollins: San Francisco, 2000.

Epstein, S., and Brodsy, A., *You're Smarter than you Think,* NewYork: Simon & Schuster, 1993.

Finch, S., *The Shame of My Ties with Hitler,* Sydney Morning Herald, 7 January 2000.

Goldberg, M.J., *The 9 Ways of Working,* Marlowe & Company: New York, 1999.

Goleman, D., *Emotional Intelligence,* London: Cox & Wyman, 1996.

Greene, R., and Elffers, J., "48 Laws of Power" Penguin Books, 1998.

Havens, S., *Comparison of Myers-Briggs and Enneagram Types of Registered Nurses,* Unpublished master's thesis, Gainesville, 1995.

Hawkins, D., *Power versus Force,* Carlsbad: Hay House, 1995.

Hoffman, R. E., *Attractor Neuro Networks and Psychotic Disorders,* PsychiatricAnnals 22:3, 119-124, 1992.

Holbrook, M.B., *Two Ways to Evaluate an Advertising Campaign,* Journal of Advertising Research, 16 (August), 45-48, 1976.

Holbrook, Morris B. and Rajeev Batra (1987), *Assessing the Role of Emotions as Mediators of Consumer Responses to Advertising,* Journal of

Consumer Research, 14 (December), 404-420.

Horney, K., *Our Inner Conflicts: A Constructive Theory of Neurosis*, New York:W.W. Norton & Company, 1945.

Howard, J., *Harding Admits Knowing of Plot After the Attack*, Washington Post, January 28, 1994.

Howard, J.A., "Consumer Behaviour: Applications of Theory" McGraw-Hill Book Co., New York, 1977.

Joseph, R., *The Naked Neuron: Evolution and the Languages of the Brain and Body*, NewYork: Plenum Publishing, 1993.

Kagan, J., *Galen's Prophecy*, NewYork: Basic Books, 1994.

Kunst-Wilson,W., and Zajonc, R.B., *Affective Discrimination of Stimuli that Cannot be Recognized*, Science, February 1980.

Lapid-Bogda, G., *Bringing Out the Best in Yourself at Work: How to Use the Enneagram System for Success*, Santa Monica: McGraw-Hill, 2004.

LeDoux, J., *Emotion and the Limbic System Concept*, Concepts in Neuroscience, 2, 1992.

LeDoux, J., *Sensory Systems and Emotion*, Integrative Psychiatry, 4, 1986.

Li, E., and Spiegel, D., *A Neuro Network Model of Associative Disorders*, PsychiatricAnnals 22:3, 144-145, 1992.

Lorenz, E.N., "Deterministic Nonperiodic Flow" Journal of Atmospheric Science 20, 130-141, 1963.

Myers, I. and McCaulley, M., *Manual: A Guide to the Development and Use of the Myer-Briggs Type Indicator*, Palo Alto: Consulting Psychologists Press, 1985.

O'Leary, P., *The Myers-Briggs and the Enneagram*, Stanford: Presentation at the First International Enneagram Conference, 1994.

Palmer, H., *The Enneagram*, San Francisco: Harper & Row, 1988.

Palmer, H., The *Enneagram Advantage: Putting the 9 Personality Types to Work in the Office*, Harmony Books: New York, 1998.

Palmer, H., *The Enneagram in Love and Work: Understanding Your Intimate & Business Relationships*, Harper/Collins: San Francisco, 1995.

Palmer, H., *Inner Knowing: Consciousness, Creativity, Insight, and Intuition*, Jeremy Tarcher/Putnam: New York, 1998.

Petty, R.E., Cacioppo, J.T., Stratham, A. J., and Priester, J. R., *To Think or not to Think*, in the book by Shavitt, S., and Brock, T, C., *Persuasion: Psychological Insights and Perspectives*, Boston: Allyn and Bacon, 1994.

Petty, R. E., and Cacioppo, J. T., *Communication and Persuasion: Central and Peripheral Routes to Attitude Change*, New York: Springer Verlag, 1986.

Reis and Trout, *Positioning*, McGraw-Hill Trade, 2000.

Riso, D.R., and Hudson, R., *Personality Types: Using the Enneagram for Self-Discovery*, Boston: Houghton Mifflin, 1996.

Snyder, K., *Nine Conflict Resolution Styles Based on the Enneagram Personality Types*, Unpublished master's thesis, Sacramento: California State University, 1996.

Thomas, K., and Kilmann, R., *Thomas-Kilmann Conflict Mode Instrument*, Tuxedo: Xicom, 1974.

Thrasher, P., *The Enneagram: Movement Between Types, an Inventory, and a Criterion Measure*, Chicago: Presentation at the First International Enneagram Conference, 1994.

Tracy, B., *Million Dollar Habits*, Eliot House Productions, 2004.

Wagner, J., *The Myers-Briggs and the Enneagram*, Stanford: Presentation at the First International Enneagram Conference, 1994.

Wagner, J.P., *Wagner Enneagram Personality Style Scales*, Los Angeles: Western Psychological Services, 1999.

Wenzlaff, R., The Mental Control of Depression, in the book, Handbook of Mental Control,Wegner and Pennebaker, 1993.

# About the Author

## Peter Burow

Peter Burow is an expert in leadership development, transformational change management and employee engagement. He is internationally regarded as a trusted advisor and expert facilitator of senior executive teams looking to drive individual, team and organisational performance. Peter has an extensive client list, including international icons such as Emirates Airline, PricewaterhouseCoopers, BHP Billiton, Xerox, Genpact and Ajinomoto.

Peter Burow

B.Bus Comm Dip. M.MHH, NS.NLP, AFAIM

Peter authored the ground breaking NeuroPower framework, a system which explains human behaviour through the integration of neuroscience, psychology and best practice management theory.

Peter is the author of numerous books, Executive Chairman of the NeuroPower Group and a Partner of a number of consulting firms that specialize in applying neuroscience, performance psychology and cultural analysis to the challenges facing leadership teams at all levels of an organization.

Peter is qualified in Business Communications, Neuroeconomics, Neurofeedback, NLP, Integral Coaching and has been awarded an honorary diploma by the Maya-Lenca people of El Salvador for his work in preserving their cultural history.

Printed in Great Britain
by Amazon

36855521R00066